IN △ PERSPECTIVE

Rosemary Hartill was born in Shropshire and read English at Bristol University. After working in publishing for six years, she became a freelance broadcaster for the BBC, and reviewed ballet and dance for the Times Educational Supplement. *In 1979 she joined the BBC as a religious affairs reporter and in 1982 was appointed Religious Affairs Correspondent in succession to Gerald Priestland, only the second woman correspondent ever to be appointed to BBC Radio UK. Since then she has travelled widely for the BBC, reporting on religion in places as far afield as the USSR, Uganda, China, Cyprus and Holland. She contributes regularly to the BBC's news services, including the World Service, and won a nomination for the 'Reporter of the Year' in the Sony Radio Awards in 1987. Recently she has been working for BBC tv's documentary series* Everyman. *An Anglican, she loves theatre and films, hill-walking and wildlife and being in Northumberland.*

IN ▶
PERSPECTIVE

Rosemary Hartill

BBC BOOKS

For the second worst birdwatcher of them all

ACKNOWLEDGEMENTS

My thanks are legion: to Alan Rogers, then Head of Current Affairs and Magazine Programmes, who first lent me a tape recorder; Anne Catchpole, who produced for *Woman's Hour* my first feature – on Channel swimming; Colin Semper of Religious Programmes, who introduced me to a BBC saltmine contract; David Winter, now Head of Religious Programmes, with whom I've spent many happy hours arguing and learning (often about theology); Gerry Priestland, who knows that a bottle of whiskey goes down a treat at evangelical conferences; Daphne Filshill, my retired and much-missed secretary, for defeating BBC bureaucracy; Frances Gumley for persuading me that Saint Teresa probably did levitate; and to all the radio producers and engineers who heard the scripts, told me when they were boring, tried to make them better, and sometimes waited in the middle of the night to receive them.

Not least, thanks to my dear parents, who kept on listening.

Published by BBC Books
A division of BBC Enterprises Ltd
Woodlands, 80 Wood Lane, London W12 0TT

First published in 1988
© BBC and Rosemary Hartill 1988
ISBN 0 563 20658 6

Photoset and printed in Great Britain by
Redwood Burn Limited, Trowbridge, Wiltshire

CONTENTS

INTRODUCTION

There's a story about an English sailor who was once shipwrecked on a desert island. It was a very desolate desert island indeed – a tiny outcrop of land separated from civilisation by thousands of miles of ocean. But on this island lived a man who spoke English, of a kind. 'Sherwisheeeswish Good morning, sir sherwishswoosh,' he said. After a while, the sailor, astonished at his good luck that anyone living in so remote a place would know any English (however bizarre its use), asked him how he learnt the language. 'Oh, soorwishsooree woooshee,' said the man, confidently. 'That's easy. Sssswishooorswush. By listening to the BBC World Service.'

That story reminds me of reporting on religion. It's like listening to something you want to hear, but which often is very faint and crackling with interference on the frequency. Retuning to another frequency may help, but even then, what's the crackle? What's the message? The correspondent has often to describe both, but also to try and indicate which is which.

The first of these selected *In Perspective* talks was broadcast in the autumn of 1982, just a few days after I was appointed the BBC's religious affairs correspondent. Another 200 or so radio talks have followed since then. Many were written under intense time pressure with the phone frequently interrupting. A few were scripted in relative leisure and calm. It seems to me that the best were when I had discovered something that mattered to me, and that I wanted to share. It could be about how to read the Old Testament without getting into a rage (*Best Bible Bits*, p 190; *We Believe* . . . , p 192); resurrection (*A Glimpse of Heaven*, p 44; *Durham Blues*, p 188); the cost of being in the church (*Partners in Crime*, p 65; *Tears and Tear-gas* p 63, *Marriage à la Mode* p 171; *Wycliffe the Unwelcome*, p 161); or finding out more about other faiths, other experiences (*If only my People* . . . , p 87; *Our Doris*, p 203). Some were reflections provoked by news stories (*Kirk's Tour*, p 13; *Synodical Games*, p 110; *And Now the News*, p 31). All show obvious signs of being prepared first for the spoken word, not the printed page. Talks I dropped from this selection were usually on subjects that had stirred in me little more than temporary interest.

In 1983, I flew to the Holy Land to see the places of Christ's life. One night I had dinner with Donald and Dorothy Nicholl at Tantur, the ecumenical institute between Bethlehem and Jerusalem. Donald was then the rector. He looks like an Old Testament prophet and writes like an angel. 'How are you enjoying your job?' he asked. 'It's very interesting . . .', I began. 'Interesting', he said, 'is not a religious concept.'

In *The Man Born To Be King*, Dorothy L. Sayers put it another way:

Not Herod, not Caiaphas, not Pilate, not Judas ever contrived to fasten upon Jesus Christ the reproach of insipidity; that final indignity was left for pious hands to inflict. To make of his story something that could neither startle, nor shock, nor terrify, nor excite, nor inspire a living soul is to crucify the Son of God afresh and put Him to open shame.

In that first *In Perspective* talk of 9 October 1982, I said that the history of Christianity and other religions has been at its heart not the history of conferences or committees, or buildings or concordats. It's been the history of individuals who've kept the light of faith burning in times of darkness. They have kept things in perspective when the tides of complacency or persecution have distracted the religions within and without. I have met some of them in my work – and my one regret is that in these pages, I have not let their beautiful voices speak more clearly.

Rosemary Hartill, BBC, Broadcasting House, 16 November 1987

CHURCH

BRITANNICA

1

In Memoriam

I was rather expecting to see in the *Church Times* this weekend a notice declaring the death of the church of England. I was ready to send the obligatory wreath of white flowers to the funeral and even thought about playing the dead march today to set the right atmosphere.

For I've been reading the latest shock horror church probe. You know, all those newspaper headlines ranging from 'Pagan Britain?' (*Daily Mail*) to 'Boring Church Faces Criticism in Poll' (*Daily Telegraph*). The story was of course the poll conducted by Gallup on behalf of the Bible Society to reveal current attitudes to the Bible, God and the church. Other cheerful headlines were 'Church under Fire' and 'Church Puts the People off Religion' (*Daily Express*). Almost 400 out of the 1,000 or so people interviewed felt apparently that the church needs to change its image if it's to attract people, and many see Christian churches as dull, uninspiring and old-fashioned.

The message to the church, it was reported, was 'have more contact with the community, increase your efforts to interest and attract young people, and aim your work more at non-attenders'. Some people criticised services as too boring, sermons as too serious, and congregations as pompous and unfriendly. So there you are, all you bishops and moderators and canons and ministers, now you know.

Well, now you know until you read the actual survey, that is.
For it seems to me that far from throwing the church into gloom
and doom, it contains some rather good news that could justify
the church's opening a bottle or two of champagne to celebrate.
For a start nearly one in six of the adult population of England
apparently goes to church at least once a week (that's more than
fifteen times the number of people who attend Football League
matches every Saturday). Even in London, one in ten goes to
church every week and reads the Bible outside those hours –
and that's the lowest figure in the whole of England.

It's not as if going to church these days was a fashionable
thing to do. Presumably all those people who go to church once
a week actually enjoy going.

In East Anglia, 28 per cent of the people questioned – that's
over one in four – go to church at least once a month. Does that
really indicate pagan Britain? Of course it doesn't. So how has
this strange myth got around?

Well, the press thrives on bad news, rather than good news,
and most of the newspapers seem to imagine that the norm in
England is a society where everyone is a paid-up church member. Secondly their negative interpretation has been encouraged by a rather downbeat news release from the Bible Society
itself. The *news release* emphasised the view of the church as
dull, uninspiring and off-putting.

I suppose that its emphasis does give moral backing to coming evangelistic campaigns supported by members of the Bible
Society. Later this year the Argentine-born evangelist Luis
Palau is visiting London, and next year Billy Graham is leading
a mission around England. The worse the state of the nation
appears to be, the greater the justification for such campaigns.

Of course, no one in the Christian churches in England
should have any room for complacency. And it's all too easy and
quite wrong to shut one's ears to complaints about the church
from people who never cross the threshold. A lot of people who
complain about Roman Catholic services, for instance, have no
idea of the enormous changes that have taken place in the style
of the Catholic liturgy over the last twenty years. Nevertheless,

it's important to recognise how people *think* things are, even if they have in fact changed. And the survey does include some disturbing facts. One that struck me particularly was that 43 per cent of people interviewed in the south-west of England said they had never read the Bible *at all* outside church services. But the fact is that 14 per cent in the same area say they read the Bible at least once a week and 11 per cent read it several times a week.

The message this tells *me* is that although the churches have a lot to do to communicate better, they've got a pretty solid base to work from.

9 July 1983

Priestly Politics

A fierce thunderstorm broke out over the centre of London yesterday, with flashes so sharp and thunder so rumbling that I began to wonder what cleric had been saying what. Not that I believe the Lord acts *quite* like that, though I see that this week's edition of *Private Eye* has a cartoon of a bishop dressed in a cassock and with a wire rod emerging from his mitre, telling a brother bishop that it's a lightning conductor.

Certainly disputes about the church and politics do get heated, as illustrated on Tuesday this week at St James's Church in London's Piccadilly. It was the launching of a collection of essays, entitled *The Church and the State*. There a Conservative MP, Mr Teddy Taylor, was explaining that he thought the church should stay out of politics because he couldn't see *any* political issue in terms of absolute right or absolute wrong. As he did so, Canon Eric James from St Albans kept on interposing questions like 'What about Auschwitz?' or 'What about apartheid?' When Mr Taylor refused to make an exception even for those, Canon James turned to the assembled company of rather bemused journalists and said he hoped we were all taking note.

You can read their respective thoughts at greater length in the book, which is based on a series of lunchtime Lent lectures delivered at St James's by a dean, a canon, a bishop, a professor and four MPs.

Professor Owen Chadwick regards the nation's heritage of 'diffused Christianity' with gratitude. Victor de Waal, the Dean of Canterbury*, wants what he calls 'critical solidarity' with the powers that be. Donald Reeves, the Rector of St James's, argues that the trappings of establishment – the bishops' palaces and so on – put a gulf between the church and many ordinary people. As a vicar on a South London housing estate, he said, it was pointless explaining that the Archbishop of Canterbury was leading a very simple life and that as an archbishop he needed premises for offices and entertainment.

But the most coherent argument in the book against the present operation of church establishment in England comes from the Bishop of Kensington, Dr Mark Santer.† The key question, he says, is not establishment itself. It's whether the church in whatever country it operates is recognised by the state as having its own inherent life, or whether in the end it is seen as the creation of the state, existing only on the terms laid down by the state. That question affects, of course, not only the churches, but all other communities within society – like trade unions, colleges, professional bodies, etc. Dr Santer argues that in at least three crucial areas – worship, subordination to the crown and general attitudes fostered within the Church of England – the church does not have a life of its own, but only a life conceded by the state. But whatever the church–state relationship, should church leaders search for so-called *Christian* policies to deal with specific *political* issues like unemployment, immigration and the rest?

Teddy Taylor argues they should not. And reminds his readers of the life of Christ. He was, he points out, living in a country ruled by an illegal colonialist regime. In the hills were a multitude of freedom fighters or political terrorists anxious to

---

* No longer at Canterbury.   † Now the Bishop of Birmingham.

cut Roman throats. There was clear discrimination in favour of Roman citizens. Yet Christ would not be drawn into urging people not to pay their taxes to this illegal colonialist regime. Nor incidentally did he advocate particular policies – instead he called people to repentance and a change of heart in their relationships with God and each other.

It seems to me that the church's problem is how to proclaim this vision of right relationships, without being so general and unspecific that its words are heard as little more than woolly waffle. Jesus, after all, nearly always spoke to particular people in particular situations. As for the Old Testament prophets, they were often highly specific in their denunciations of the actions of the rulers of the day. They make our own Christian leaders sound mealy-mouthed. Part of their wider perspective was always goodness to the stranger and help to the poor, the widowed, the orphan and the hungry. That's why Eric James refuses to concentrate on narrow church–state relations, but writes about Christian responsibility to the wider world.

David Steele, the leader of the Liberal Party, quotes the Magnificat – Mary's song of praise to the Lord God. 'He hath put down the mighty from their seats, and exalted them of low degree. He hath filled the hungry with good things; and the rich he hath sent empty away.' Little wonder – he says – that George Bernard Shaw thought the Magnificat more revolutionary than the Internationale, that according to Dante, Robert, King of Sicily, ordered it to be sung only in Latin, and that for the same reason it is today banned in several South American countries as being too subversive.

6 October 1984

Kirk's Tour

Each year towards the end of May in the gloomy but imposing Presbyterian High Kirk of Edinburgh's St Giles's Cathedral, the establishment of Scotland attends morning service. The images are like a kaleidoscope – gowns, medals, maces, processions, sunlight slanting through the strong stained glass, stalwart Gothic columns in pink and grey stone. There's the Queen's representative, the Lord High Commissioner, and the city council, people from the university and the judiciary. Judges in wigs and red and white silk. And the choir in red gowns with high collars standing up at the back of their heads. They are all there to join in worship with the 1,250 ministers and elders who have gathered in Edinburgh from all over Scotland for the Church of Scotland's General Assembly.

For though the influence of the assembly has much declined over the last fifty years, it still remains the nearest thing Scotland has to its own parliament. Its moderator this year is the Right Reverend Dr David Smith. His sermon at St Giles's urged Christians to get on the march to resist what he believes to be a great campaign to destroy the Christian heritage of Britain. The situation, he said, even resembled that of Germany in the 1930s. When pressed by puzzled journalists to explain exactly what he meant, he declined. The trouble with moderators, as with bishops, to quote someone else, is that generally speaking they tend to be generally speaking.

As for the assembly itself, it was soon far too busy passing resolutions – or deliverances as they are known – to worry about all that. Most members only attend the annual assembly once every four years. So it's as if there's a compulsion to deliver as many opinions in one week as a parliament might take over four years. We had everything from a declaration in favour of a nuclear freeze to one encouraging people to install and wear seat belts in the back seats of cars.

On social issues the assembly swung towards a much harder line on abortion, favouring a ban except when the mother's life was in danger. It rejected the idea of any experimentation at all on human embryos. On matters to do with church government, it settled several judicial cases where a minister had fallen out with his congregation, and it discussed relations with other denominations.

The latest news about membership, incidentally, is that now

less than 600,000 people attend the communion service once a year or more, and the kirk's finances and problems with buildings are still difficult. But generally the mood seemed more optimistic and confident than twelve months ago. You may remember that last year there was a terrific row in the women's guild over a theological report exploring the motherhood of God. The report was criticised rather more than it was read, and thrown out by the assembly in an ill-mannered fashion. This year the women's guild presented the blandest of faces, intent on forgetting all that was past.

Altogether about 800 deliverances were passed. Quite why the kirk – and so many other Protestant assemblies in the British Isles – goes in for passing so many resolutions is becoming a mystery to me. Their effect on government policy certainly seems to be minimal, except in their long-term influence on public opinion and voting patterns. Yet the enthusiasm for this system continues. One very experienced party political worker observing the assembly told me he was amazed at how little lobbying the church goes in for, to press home the message of these resolutions. My impression is that the churches are more willing to lobby than before, but are still rather amateur at the business.

One of the most interesting debates this time was about the proposals towards a united church of Scotland, consisting of the Church of Scotland and five other Protestant denominations. These were given a welcome by not a very large majority and referred to the presbyteries for discussion. The main hurdle is the Presbyterian suspicion that bishops are to be slipped into the church by a back door in the guise of long-term moderators. It was yet another reminder that church structures are just as much of an obstacle to progress towards church unity as doctrine. At the root of this is the whole question of authority. Presbyterians are passionately proud of their democratic style of government. Some fear that if they accept anything approaching a two-tiered ministry – bishops and the rest – they are on the slippery slope towards hierarchical government on the Roman model. Others are saying, 'Look, all we are suggest-

ing is that some moderators hold their job for seven years rather than just one. And we believe this will provide better support and help for hard-pressed ministers.' At next year's assembly we shall discover whether the local presbyteries are convinced.*
25 May 1985

Priests Alarmed

Fashion shows of ecclesiastical night attire don't usually feature much in a journalist's life. But I can now disclose that at least one Roman Catholic archbishop goes to bed wearing bright pink pyjamas, and that one priest possibly even wears a trilby hat. I know this because at two o'clock last Wednesday morning, a deafening fire alarm sounded at Newman College, Birmingham, and within minutes 150 Roman Catholic priests and bishops, and assorted journalists, tumbled out of their beds down to the safety of the grassy courtyard below. It turned out to be a false alarm, which was just as well for the priest who slept through the lot.

The priests were attending the annual National Conference of Roman Catholic priests in England and Wales, and this year the subject was the priest's role in a violent world. The priests are on the whole a cheerful, sociable group of men. They avoided wasting time just denouncing other people's actions. But each of them had experienced violence in their ministry – whether it was teaching in a Glasgow classroom, or coping with broken families and broken areas in other cities and towns. One priest told the conference that of the fellow students he had trained with in America, six had now been murdered. The purpose of the conference was for people to share their experiences, to provide encouragement for those who were downhearted, support for those who were under pressure, and a challenge to any who were complacent.

---

* They weren't.

The organised challenge came in the form of three talks: Bishop Kelly of Salford spoke on the theology of suffering, Monsignor Bruce Kent of CND spoke of the dangers of the church absorbing the values of the status quo of the day, and Father Austin Smith described his experience of inner city violence in Liverpool.

The theme that linked all three speeches was in effect a call to the church to be more religious. Each of the three contributors, along with their listeners, would interpret slightly differently what that meant in practice. But what came through was a vision of a Christian community, living in the middle of a violent world, but nevertheless showing what a non-violent, loving and free community inspired by the gospel, *can* be like.

Each speaker indicated some of the things that were holding the church back. Bishop Kelly said the teaching of the church was meant not to make people captive, but to give them freedom and fullness of life. Bruce Kent believed that in countries all round the world, and in century after century, the church had too often fallen into the trap of providing spiritual support for the state's sometimes violent policies, rather than a non-violent critique of them. Father Smith appealed both to politicians and the church to stop thinking that merely *listening* to people was enough. Just going round saying you were listening to them and then going away and talking about them was, he implied, a cop out, because it wasn't a real conversation. It was a dangerous cop out, too, because it made people angry.

The questioning of authority implied by these and other statements may have made some conservative priests uncomfortable. But the old-style, traditional priests don't usually go in for attending conferences like this one. And there was a general feeling that the church itself had all too often much to answer for. Religion, as one priest said, is not usually associated with the word peace, at least to outsiders who over the centuries have watched people killing each other in the name of religion. One of the final resolutions specifically expressed concern over violence in the church itself – what it called 'the exercise of authority *at any level*, which submitted the church's members to moral or psychological violence'. The words 'at any level' clearly include the Pope himself. For the conference went on to uphold the right of theologians to legitimate enquiry and speculation. This, they said, should be encouraged as essential to the life of the church. They had, it seems, especially in mind Father Leonardo Boff, the Brazilian theologian, who has been temporarily silenced by the Vatican.

It has to be said that among this group of English and Welsh priests, just as among their bishops, the present way in which the Vatican is exercising some of its power was not being very warmly received. And they hoped Cardinal Hume, of Westminster would say so with effect at the extraordinary synod of bishops to be held in Rome in late November.

7 September 1985

Laying in Wait

I have discovered this week that one way of getting a pay rise if you're a minister is to move into a house next door to a crematorium. Methodist ministers reckon that fees for conducting funerals once or twice a week can produce an extra £2,000 a year on their salary. That curious little fact lay nestled in the 784 pages of the agenda of the Methodist Conference – Methodism's governing body – which is meeting this week in Birmingham. As usual there were reports on this and that and everything from the running of the Methodist Homes for the Aged to whether boxing should be discouraged, and whether the church should take out insurance against professional negligence. Could this be in case a particularly bad preacher finally bores someone to death? No, it has, it seems, more to do with professional cover for advice concerning church property.

But the Methodist agenda also revealed that the church is short of ministers. One world-wide response from Methodists, Anglicans, Roman Catholics and others to a shortage of clergy is to try to encourage lay people to take more responsibility for the life of the local church.

In places like Latin America and Africa some parishes now have over 100,000 members. In response so-called 'basic communities' have developed – small groups of Christians within the parish who worship and study together and who share each other's lives.

Just recently I've been travelling around England a fair bit. And I do have the impression that most churchgoers still regard the church as the responsibility of the ordained clergy. One trenchant parochial church council member I talked to recently described the moves within the Church of England to change that view as 'plans to get the laity to do the clergy's job for them'. That attitude is changing, but it dies hard.

Over the last fifteen years, Anglican leaders have tried hard to get the laity more involved in the running of the Church of England. The establishment of the new system of synodical government in 1970, where lay people take an active role, was part of that plan. And in most parishes these days, lay people regularly read the lesson, help to distribute communion and so on. But in the way the various synods operate, there's a tendency for accountants, business people, teachers and other middle-class professionals to run the various church committees rather in the style they might go about their *secular* work. It's as if they feel they know about committees, but are uncomfortable when it comes to anything more 'religious', like leading the liturgy, or helping out with the regular visiting, or organising meetings for doubters anonymous who want to find out more about what Christians really believe.

In some country parishes with diminishing populations, the problem is intense. For some years now the church has been unable to provide a separate priest for each parish. Instead priests have had to try to look after two, three or more parishes. Yet it has been rare for the lay people to step forward and take full responsibility for their local church. One church I attended in a village in Wiltshire had three people apart from myself in the congregation. The vicar did everything himself – played the organ, led the singing, read the lessons and saw us out. In another church in Northumberland, there was only one other member of the congregation at evensong. The vicar preached a marvellous sermon, but where were the people to hear it? Another beautiful church I visited has a service normally once a month.

At a recent international conference I attended in Belgium, a French Roman Catholic bishop described similar problems in his diocese. He had discovered, he said, that while a parish still has a priest – even if the priest is nominally caring for several other parishes at once – the laity don't take on responsibility for the life of the church. So now when a priest dies, the bishop doesn't appoint a new one. The congregation come to see him, angrily saying it is his job to provide a priest. He waits for them to have their say, and then he tells them he has made the decision because he respects them, because he believes their faith and gifts are strong enough for *them* to be the church in their village. His diocese now provides effective training for such lay people and after a while he appoints a priest to support several such parishes in that area. This, he suggests, helps keep the local communities in touch with the wider church, and of course the priest can celebrate the Mass as necessary. It's a radical step. But one that in his experience is working.

29 June 1985

St Elsewhere's Cathedral

Not so long ago I listened in to a guided tour of one of the great English cathedrals. A group of tourists was being whisked round at high speed and served a cocktail of dates, architectural facts and a few anecdotes about those whose mortal remains lie beneath the floors. There was no time allowed for prayer, or even for a peaceful contemplation of the majesty of the building, before the party was being hustled off back to the bus *en route* to the next tourist site.

A week or two later I was lucky enough to be shown round another cathedral by a friend who worships there each week. It was Durham, where at the east end lie the last remains of one of the saints of the English church, St Cuthbert. By the end of our tour I had a real sense of being part of a church living through the ages.

How can the people who run cathedrals try to share some of that sense of continuity with the millions who visit them each year?

Well, this week I attended a conference organised by the Cathedrals and Churches Pilgrims Association. Over seventy deans, provosts, guides, vergers and educational advisers were discussing how best to welcome the ever-growing numbers of visitors.

There was a lot of talk about providing good clear guide-books, loos and parking, about organising concerts and special services, about encouraging the local press to run regular stories on what the cathedral is doing, so that more people will want to come and visit. But when all's said and done, what are the people really supposed to be coming for? Is it just to marvel at the glories of English architecture and to observe from the sidelines somebody else's act of worship? Or is it to feel here in this place part of something amazing that is going on that just can't be found anywhere else? One of the deans said to me that a cathedral should in one sense be a monastery at prayer. The conversation left me wondering why, in that case, so many cathedrals *don't* feel like a monastery at prayer. Why is it, for instance, that cathedral chapters have a reputation for in-fighting and petty arguments? Why is it that some cathedral staff give visitors the impression that they are welcoming them on sufferance? Why do cathedrals sometimes close the building for special services without putting up notices explaining to visitors exactly what is going on, and asking for their prayers?

The answers are legion. One theory is that part of the blame should be laid at the feet of that arch-wrecker Henry VIII. Before the Reformation, religious communities would have been attached to the cathedrals as a matter of course. When

Henry dissolved the monasteries, a whole tradition of English contemplative prayer was smashed. Today it survives in fragments in communities around the country, but it has never regained its spiritual influence.

The bureaucracy of many cathedrals is now so rigid that it is, I am afraid, a pipe dream to hope that the religious communities could be invited back to the cathedrals as a normal part of their worshipping life. But some things can be done and are being done. In the old days, a cathedral was regarded as the mother church of the diocese. Christians from the area would go to visit the cathedral much as you go home every now and then to visit your mother. Yet so often parishes these days seem to have hardly any links with the cathedral.

At the conference the Very Reverend John Allen, the Provost of Wakefield, described how in his area he's trying to put that right. In the past two years about a third of the parishes in the Wakefield diocese have visited the cathedral. What he does is to invite a parish party for a day out. The party go off to visit a nearby beauty spot, then arrive at the cathedral with their sandwiches. They are welcomed with tea and orangeade and the group stay on to share evensong. If necessary one of the cathedral staff takes the normal service at the parish church back home for those unable to join the trip. The provost says he hopes it helps parishes to renew their links with the cathedral as the mother church and to feel part of a wider worshipping community.

Of course it's not easy to run a cathedral and some staff do a marvellous job given the overwhelming number of visitors. But a great many people who will come to a cathedral would never go near an ordinary church. If they don't have a sense of prayer and of Christian life being lived out there, then no wonder the tour operators whisk people round the cathedral just as if it were any other tourist spot.

28 September 1985

Back to Buckhaven

Imagine going along one day to your local fish and chip shop for a takeaway. You're queueing, when one of the older customers turns to the local minister who's also there and starts taking him to task for changing the life of the church so much that it doesn't seem to be the church she remembers any more. Then a couple of lads in black leather jackets enter the argument to say that she should leave him alone. The church, they say, has really got things going in the town and thanks to that, they've now got a future.

That argument took place not so long ago in the Scottish town of Buckhaven, where three years ago the Church of Scotland congregation set out on an adventure in job creation which grew and grew. The church is at the centre of a series of schemes financed by the Community Programme or the Youth Training Schemes of the Manpower Services Commission (MSC). About 750 people are now employed either full- or part-time. Every week, the minister, the Reverend Dane Sherrard, handles weekly pay cheques amounting to nearly £35,000. When the chairman of MSC in Scotland, Sir James Munn, visited Buckhaven at the end of last year, he described the project as a remarkable success story – a unique achievement. Of its kind, he said, this project ranked among the best in Britain, providing a future for so many people in a difficult employment area. When you see it, it's hard not to be impressed.

Buckhaven is a small town on the east coast of Fife about an hour's drive from Edinburgh. It was a sparkling sunny day when I was there earlier this week, and a number of oil rigs were stationed squarely in the bay waiting for repairs further up the coast. The town, which has a population of about 8,000, started life as a fishing village, with a later interest in weaving. But once local mining began, the harbour silted up and the fish moved away. After a series of accidents several pits were closed. By 1983, two out of five men of working age were out of work.

It was that year that the church first thought up a scheme to convert a former church building into an arts and crafts centre for people with time on their hands.

Before long they got money through the Community Programme agency for 116 jobs. They deliberately chose people who had been out of work for a long time. Dane Sherrard says that at first everyone was excited about the building. But it wasn't long before they realised that what was important wasn't the building, but the work that was being created: the money circulating in the shops, the marriages no longer breaking up now that the pressure of unemployment had been removed, the holidays that were possible, the new curtains appearing at people's windows – signs of hope and pride.

But the church project is now just one of over forty in the town. And one of the striking things is the imaginativeness of the range of the projects. It's hard these days to get theatrical costumes from anywhere nearer than Manchester. So one group is busy learning how to make costumes. In the same room, others are enjoying doing clothes alterations for local people. There are other workshops ranging from boat-building to weaving to book-binding. Everybody's favourite project is the so-called miracle room upstairs. Here a group of men are building props for stage magicians – vanishing boxes and guillotines from which the magician's assistant miraculously emerges alive. These can be used to entertain children and adults, and raise money for local charities. The project could one day be a business in its own right as these days the nearest place to Buckhaven you can buy such full-size stage illusions is Hamburg, I'm told. Overall, 15 per cent of jobs are said to be taken by disabled people.

It's hard to draw lessons for other congregations who are tempted to set up similar schemes. Not all church projects for people out of work have been successful. So much depends on leadership, the level of commitment, and whether real trust is built up between the church and non-churchgoers. For those who fear that the Buckhaven project is more like a secular community scheme than a church, Dane Sherrard replies that the effect on the spiritual life of the church has been 'wonderful'. Most members of the congregation would not, it seems, share the unease of the woman in the fish and chip shop.

20 September 1986

Bread and Stones

I was chatting to a priest this week who was talking about why when millions of people in this country go to church regularly many more millions don't. He said he once had a lodger in his house, a young man who never showed the slightest interest in the church. He lived for four years in a vicarage directly opposite the building without ever entering it, except once for a concert. When he was a small boy his mother had said to him, 'If you are naughty, I shall send you to Sunday school.' So he made sure he was never that naughty. He told the priest that he couldn't think why at 9.30 on a Sunday morning when all civilised people were in bed, some should want to go for an hour to that cold and draughty building, sit on hard seats and listen to him. The priest had to admit that put like that, and if that was all worship was, then he couldn't either! And he reckoned that out of the 20,000 people who lived in his parish, the lodger represented the thinking of about 19,700 of them.

One difficulty is that if you go to church, there's pressure to join in everything. What happens if you don't believe all the items of the creed? If you recite all the words you feel a hypocrite. Then there's a sense of feeling trapped. Nearly everyone I've ever met has some terrible tale to tell about a disastrous sermon they've heard. I had such an experience a week or so back when I was attending a harvest festival in the countryside. The sermon began with pointing out that most of the world's wealth was concentrated in the hands of a few. But after that there was no discussion about what those listening could or should do to deal with a sense of anxiety about this. There were no practical suggestions. Instead the sermon meandered off into generalities about creation. At the end of it all, I felt I had come asking for bread and been handed a stone. But there was no way of conveying this, however politely, except by never going to hear the same preacher again. One of my friends has made that decision, in different churches, every week for the last nine weeks.

How can communication be improved? Well, the priest who told me the story about his lodger said that for a three-month period in his church, the congregation decided to applaud the sermon to indicate to the preacher what they thought of it. It was at times, he said with a grin, a salutary experience.

Another idea is one taken up by a priest in the Russian Orthodox Church in Moscow. He asked people to send in questions about faith beforehand and to meet after the service when he answered the questions. The scheme was so successful, with so many people attending, that the Soviet authorities had him moved out of the parish. He ended up later in gaol. Some parishes have set up agnostics anonymous groups. In these meetings people who are still at a stage when they feel uncomfortable in the worship, can have a chance to get off their chests what they want to say, and then move on from there.

Not every priest can be a good preacher. Some priests who are honest about this encourage members of the congregation to take lay ministry courses, so that they can preach. Some ministers do a marvellous job in the pulpit, making sure they relate their sermons carefully to the biblical lessons read, and trying to meet the real needs of the congregation. I remember once arriving at evensong at a tiny village church in Northumberland. Most Christians in the village attended the morning service, but one person in particular liked evensong. So the priest carried on with the service, sometimes preaching only to him. The day I was there, the congregation numbered three. But the vicar had prepared a fine sermon, which I still treasure to this day. But why is it this happens so rarely?

18 October 1986

Home Truths

One of my first memories of working for the BBC was hearing from one of the secretaries how, the day before, a male producer had walked into a room containing three women and said cheerfully, 'Oh there's no one here', and walked out again. This struck me as almost as funny as watching someone come in the day after and announce that H.R.P.R. wanted the R.O.T. Sometime later when I'd got used to the BBC habit of talking in initials, I discovered this meant that the Head of Religious Programmes, Radio (H.R.P.R.) wanted to hear the tape of a programme recorded off transmission (R.O.T.).

Of course every organisation you ever come across has its jargon and its quirky ways. Not least those church committee meetings, whether in parishes, presbyteries or circuits, where conversations range from whether the scoutmaster's name should be allowed on the church notice-board to the theological views of John Calvin. The odd thing is that any human meeting, whether it's a BBC committee, a presbytery, or a political party conference, has a tendency to divide into arguing factions. That is, until the common enemy is perceived, and then for a while there's a shuffling together to produce a united front.

But *should* church meetings be like any other meetings you might attend? Talk to anyone who's sat on a church committee and they will, usually with a laugh, be able to recall stories of how people have used moral blackmail, rhetoric, manipulation, even sulking to try to further their own viewpoint. This is the subject of many ironic jokes in private, but this week the principal of an Anglican theological college has been honest enough to discuss it openly. In the Annual Sermon given to the Church Missionary Society, Ruth Etchells, the principal of St John's College with Cranmer Hall in Durham, criticised the Church of England for being 'spiritually poverty-stricken' in its life as a community. She emphasised that although church people in their private lives often tried to live close to the example of Christ, as a group they showed what she called an 'extraordinary unscrupulous worldliness'. The church's own spiritual poverty in its life as a community, she suggested, was the main reason why the church spoke with so little authority to the desperate spiritual poverty of the world.

The theme of her sermon came from some words of St Paul calling Christians to live their earthly lives in preparing for the time when they will become citizens of heaven. If Christians really took that to heart, every meeting would be transformed. Probably the Society of Friends treats it most seriously. When they are unable to resolve a difference of opinion, they quietly begin to pray, then return to the discussion. No decision is taken until a consensus is reached by *all* present through the help of prayer.

Miss Etchell's sermon was written long before the statement last week by the Bishop of London about a possible split in the Church of England, but her words obviously have some relevance to it. The bishop, Dr Graham Leonard, was warning that if the General Synod goes ahead with the ordination of women priests, then the end result could be two separate Churches of England. The archbishops are not commenting. As for others, some people have welcomed what they regard as the bishop's honesty in giving voice to the feelings of some priests and lay people, and making it plain that those who oppose women priests will not necessarily either just go over to Rome or eventually get used to the idea. Other Christians feel that the talk of two separate churches amounts to moral blackmail. Certainly those who talk about a possible separated church are extremely vague about the practical details.

They say they would hope for a negotiated settlement, but it's hard to see how the church could negotiate the sharing-out of church buildings. Buildings after all have congregations who don't want to be shifted elsewhere to worship. Then there's the question of how many people really share the bishop's views. Though perhaps several hundred priests might feel sympathetic, it is quite another question as to how many would, when it came to it, really want two separate churches. And it's thought no more than a handful of bishops out of well over a hundred would contemplate joining.

Perhaps all those who are involved in this argument – whatever their views – pro or anti women priests – might reflect on Ruth Etchell's sermon.

5 October 1985

More Home Truths

Annual reports – whether school, business or society reports – aren't exactly a ripping good read. And the annual report produced this week by the Methodist Church's Home Mission Division is no exception. But it is attractively designed, is intended to encourage rather than impress its readers, and dares to call itself *Home Truths*.

It is frank enough to suggest that the village Methodist and the village chapel are in some areas an endangered species and a threatened habitat. But it goes on to present a series of pictures of Methodists at work elsewhere – ranging from chaplains in the armed forces to those working with drug addicts – which show that Methodism is still alive and well.

There is, for instance, the portrait of the Methodist minister who works with some of the 130,000 Chinese in this country. And the inner city church at Clapton Park in London which now attracts thirty-five men to a weekly prayer and Bible study meeting. Then there is the centre in the Manchester area for young people who are trying to kick the drugs habit. All this work is going on quietly and unpretentiously.

But over the last few years, there's a feeling among Methodists in some parts that Methodism has in a sense lost its way. It certainly retains many faithful ministers, preachers and congregations, but there's an impression of a slight loss of confidence, a treading of old paths out of habit rather than conviction, a lack of clear goals for the future.

Some Christians of other denominations talk as if Methodists don't have much clear theology. But to Methodists, the Methodist hymn book is rather like the missal is to Roman Catholics. Week in, week out, they sing the hymns of Charles Wesley, until the theology of those hymns almost breathes from their bones. Methodists don't put great barriers around their communion table – they welcome to it all who love the Lord Jesus Christ. But Wesley's hymns, and the hymns of other Methodist writers, are packed with an intense understanding of the sacrifice of Christ's death. There is almost a mysticism about Methodist prayer and belief, which often makes them closer in spirit to Roman Catholics than Anglicans.

Getting closer to Christians of other denominations has of course been an aim of many Methodist leaders this century. The present and former General Secretaries of the World Council of Churches, for instance, are both Methodists. And the British Council of Churches has been staunchly supported by Methodists through some shaky times. Over the last few years the Methodist Church has twice been prepared to sign unity agreements with the Anglican. But in each case the Church of England has jilted the Methodists at the altar. One question hovering around the Home Mission report, but not quite faced by it, is where does the church go now in relation to other denominations?

Of course some Methodists believe that the problem is that Methodist congregations have over the years become too like Anglicans. They argue that if Methodism had kept true to the original inspiration of its founder John Wesley, it would have been an order of wandering evangelists within the Church of England – a sort of ginger group, rooted in holiness, but challenging the wider church to feed the hungry and visit the sick, and helping local lay people *become* the church themselves.

To help people understand what the Bible taught, Wesley organised numerous Bible study and prayer meetings. These eighteenth-century prayer groups were very similar to the sort of Christian groups springing up today in many parts of the Third World, called basic Christian communities.

Where·British Methodism goes to in the next few years, God knows. And most Methodists will be quite happy to leave it at that. But the signs are that in some country areas, as the chapels have quietly closed, a number of remaining Methodists may go back to the Church of England. In the Home Mission's report, perhaps the toughest home truth is that given by Alan Davies, chairman of the Lincoln and Grimsby District. He says that village Christians should worship wherever possible in the village, even if that means going to the Anglican parish church. He accepts that this will cause offence to some Methodists, but in the battle for the countryside, he says, the old denominational labels have lost much of their meaning.

11 January 1986

And Now the News

On Thursday this week my boss, Dr Colin Morris, Head of BBC Religious Broadcasting (now Controller of BBC Northern Ireland), gave the annual Hibbert lecture on Radio 4 on 'Why is there not much more good news on television? Why all the doom and gloom?' In his experience, that's the most frequently asked question at BBC public meetings. And the applause that invariably greets this question suggests there's a raw nerve here.

One reason, he said, there's so much bad news is that TV news editors still recognise that the baseline of our world is a happy, well-adjusted society. What disturbs that norm is news. We should really start getting worried if a news bulletin announced that a plane had landed safely at Gatwick today. For that would imply most planes didn't land safely.

The lecture set me reflecting on the problem of news reporting in relation to religious ideas. And I began wondering how today's journalists, had we been working in the first century, would have reported on the meetings held by St Paul. Take Paul's visit to Ephesus. I rather imagine that the news desk of the *Empire Times* or the Roman Broadcasting Corporation would have seen it as a trade union and law and order story. Imagine the headline, 'Jewish Sect Provokes Riot'. The story might have run like this:

Several thousand Ephesian trade unionists this morning demonstrated against a Jewish sect which they believe is threatening their livelihood. The workers belong to the guild of silversmiths who make shrines for the goddess Diana. Their president, Demetrius, criticised a wandering preacher called Paul who claimed that gods made with human hands were not gods at all. Two of Paul's colleagues were shouted down when they tried to speak. For two hours the workers chanted 'Great is Diana of the Ephesians.'

The report might have gone on to describe Paul as a follower of a vagrant Galilean peasant who was crucified for stirring up political trouble. His followers claimed that he performed miracles and exorcisms, and that he rose from the dead. The sect, we might be told, denies allegations of cannibalism.

That story reveals several of the characteristics of a modern-day news story. For a start, it deals with what is new, it packs a lot into a short space and it's concerned with concrete factual events rather than ideas. The question is, can this style of reporting seriously communicate theological ideas? If not, should the church give up on the secular press and concentrate on its own channels of communication – the pulpit, the church press and its own broadcasting stations?

That's the viewpoint taken by some people working, for instance, in the Vatican press office itself. It's a fortress mentality, which has led in some cases to a thinly veiled mutual contempt between some Vatican employees and Italian journalists. And some of the Vatican attempts to communicate are bizarre. A recent Vatican document urged priests to learn a lesson from Christ, the perfect communicator who always spoke in the language of ordinary people. Yet the entire document was couched in ecclesiastical Latinate Vaticanese. Are we, one begins to ask, in Lewis Carroll's Wonderland?

One of the problems it seems to me is that many religious

people have an unrealistic idea of the national press, confusing it with what I believe should be the role of the religious press. A secular newspaper is a business providing news. If Bishop X or Moderator Y has views which are apparently out of step with orthodox church opinion and which upset a number of the faithful, that's news. To complain, as some Christians do, that the news outlets do not give similar space to the orthodox views of Bishop A is beside the point.

Of course journalists sometimes get into a big muddle over religious stories. They are used to dealing mostly with facts. When the normal factual framework of reporting has suddenly to cope with ideas and beliefs expressed symbolically, the strain is sometimes intense. We are expected not only to understand exactly what the theologian means and grasp the religious truth of it, but then to summarise it and get the heart of the message across simply to the reader, listener or viewer.

This week some news outlets reported that the Bishop of Durham had said God was not exclusively male. Why on earth is this a news story, you may ask? Why is it that news desks don't seem to know that God is above gender? One answer is that it's yet another sign of the gulf between what many people think Christian teaching is and what it actually is. And for that, the church has very largely itself to blame.

27 September 1986

Des. Res. – Bishop's Palace

One of my favourite stories about the appointment of bishops goes back to 1880, when the diocese of Liverpool was created. The first bishop was Bishop Ryle, a very convinced low church Anglican. He was appointed by Queen Victoria and the Prime Minister, Disraeli, to annoy the leader of the opposition, Gladstone, who was a high churchman. Compared with that, the news this week that Mrs Thatcher merely chose as next Bishop of Birmingham the second of two

names offered to her by the Crown Appointments Commission
seems pretty small beer indeed. For in doing so, she was merely
exercising her right as agreed between church and state in 1977.
Since that date, diocesan bishops in the Church of England are
appointed like this: two names are put forward by the commission, whose voting members include the archbishops of York
and Canterbury and ten other Anglicans. The Prime Minister
may forward to the Queen either or neither of the names – for
the Prime Minister may in theory ask the commission for other
names if neither suits, though it's thought that this right has
never been exercised.

Most church members see that system as a great improve-
ment on the previous one when the Prime Minister had a free
hand in recommending appointments to the monarch. But
what would happen if a future Prime Minister of whatever party
refused to nominate *any* bishops who did not share the same
political views? Or if the Prime Minister were a convinced
atheist, intent on weakening the church's leadership? For these
reasons, some Christians argue, reform is needed. But what
would be a better system?

Well, the book of Acts includes a warning story of what not to
do. After the defection of Judas, the remaining eleven apostles
chose his successor Matthias by drawing lots. Nothing was
heard of him ever again. God's choice, it seems, was St Paul,
who was never elected by any human being. But generally in the
first centuries of the church, the local congregations elected
their bishops, choosing men who were holy, loved, and would
be good leaders. In Milan in 374, the people elected as bishop
the prefect of the city – the mayor. Legend has it he was not
even a deacon, never mind a priest. In vain did he plead his
unsuitability. Within a week he was baptised and consecrated
bishop. This incredible candidate was so loved that he was
eventually declared a saint, St Ambrose.

After a while, to make things a little easier, the lay people
were represented by parliaments, and nobles, and monarchs.
But in some places kings started appointing their favourites or
their sons as bishops. This was one cause of various church–

state quarrels in Europe in the Middle Ages and later. In several countries these were resolved by church–state agreements. Under the 1802 French concordat signed by Napoleon, the local governments in Alsace and Lorraine still recommend nominees for a diocese. But in most places the Pope chooses his new bishops on the advice of the Vatican's diplomatic corps.

There are various other systems – the Eastern orthodox bishops are chosen by other bishops, who are all monks and celibate. But in practice, there has often been government influence, in places like Greece and the Soviet bloc. In some sister churches of the Church of England as in North America or New Zealand, bishops are elected by representatives of the diocese, but have to be confirmed by a majority of the bishops. On occasion, that's led to stalemate, compromise candidates and long delays. It's another sign that no system is perfect.

11 April 1987

THE CHRISTIAN WORLD

2

The Wide, Wide World

The last postcard's been sent, the last hug's been given, and within a few hours, the final traces of the huge World Council of Churches Assembly in Vancouver will have gone. All except a worn patch of grass where the vast yellow and white worship tent was once filled with so much music and prayer in praise of God. In cities and villages all round the world, the three thousand or so people who took part are arriving back home, looking ruefully at the bags of dirty washing and sitting down at the kitchen table to describe what it was all like.

There's Frieda Haddad, the former social worker from Lebanon who goes back to a city where one day she may be a victim of the bombs. Domitila Barrios from Bolivia, back home with her eight children and her husband who's a tin miner working long hours. Or Mother Euphrasia, who returns to her monastic community in Rumania. At every Christian festival her monastery is thronged with men and women from the towns and villages. She wears the Orthodox high flat black hat and dress, and she and her sisters pray in turns day and night for the church and the world. And then there's the Scots headmaster, Harry Ashmall, whose experience in dealing firmly but humorously with Bolshie kids, is useful practice in coping with the occasional tantrum in ecclesiastical committees.

I rather suspect that around the various kitchen tables this morning there'll be stories about the people they met and the worship they shared, rather than a rush to describe the conference resolutions.

For, as usual, the World Council ended its proceedings with a flurry of documents and statements. They ranged from outlines of broad principles of human rights and justice and peace, to resolutions on specific areas of the world. For instance, it called for a Middle East settlement that took account of the plight of the Palestinians, condemned nuclear weapons and called for economic sanctions against South Africa.

American policy in Central America was soundly condemned – with, I may say, the support of most of the American delegates. But after national tensions flared, the most that emerged on Afghanistan was a carefully worded compromise statement. It backed UN efforts to work for an end to the supply of arms to opposition groups from outside the country and for the withdrawal of Russian troops. The withdrawal would be in the context of an overall political settlement, including agreement between Afghanistan and the USSR. At least one of the Russian church people understood this to mean the safeguarding of the Socialist Republic in Afghanistan.

Interestingly some people who had no liking *at all* for the Russian presence there, thought the statement usefully realistic. But I have to say that realism was not a feature of some other statements. Even if there were an international law banning nuclear weapons, for instance, how could you verify that it was not being broken? And do statements which seem to take little regard of Israel's concerns, really encourage Mr Begin to negotiate with the PLO as well as Arab governments in the area?

This raises the interesting question of what is the aim of assembly statements anyway? Is it to proclaim a Christian ideal or vision? Or is it to try to create the sort of climate where things can be moved a step closer towards the ideal? The Bishop of Durham, Dr John Habgood,* argued for realism, but the

---

* Now Archbishop of York.

World Council style – under its present General Secretary anyway – is mostly prophecy. The effect of this prophecy can be a little diminished when you know that for some delegates the freedom to attend has to some extent curtailed the freedom of speech. And when you know too that generalised resolutions are being voted on by people who perhaps have less than complete access to all information.

But the World Council of Churches has provided moral support and prayer for Christians who desperately need it, it has opened hearts and minds, it has worked faithfully for theological convergence and not just social action. And if it didn't exist, something of the sort would have to be invented. I am glad to know that somewhere in the heart of Rumania, Mother Euphrasia and her nuns are praying, perhaps right now, for Frieda Haddad in the Lebanon, Harry Ashmall in Scotland, and Domitila Barrios in Bolivia. And maybe even for you and me.

13 August 1983

Shanghai Morning

As this talk goes out, I hope to be 5,500 miles away on the other side of the globe, recording a group of Christians at a lively service of thanksgiving in a community church in Shanghai. Singing along with the local congregation will be the Archbishop of Canterbury, Dr Runcie, the General Secretary of the British Council of Churches, Dr Philip Morgan, and eighteen other representatives of the British and Irish churches. The service in Shanghai is a service of thanksgiving for the reopening of relations after more than thirty years of almost no communication. So if the archbishop and the rest can fend off jet lag, it should be quite an occasion.

People in the west are sometimes surprised there *are* still any Christians in China, what with the atheist philosophy of the state and the excesses of the Cultural Revolution. In 1966 the

Red Guard youth groups led spontaneous attacks against all visible forms of religion, as part of their criticism of what were known as 'The Four Olds' (old habits, old customs, old ideas and old culture). Muslim mosques, Christian churches and Buddhist temples were closed, sacked or turned into factories or storehouses. Individuals lost Bibles and all religious literature. Some clergy were arrested, some sent to labour camps, some died. The churches were indeed weak – the congregation a scattered flock.

But today, there seems to be a cautious liberalisation. Government campaigns against Chinese *folk* religion are still pursued, and according to the *World Christian Encyclopedia*, over half the population is now indifferent to religion. But the same source estimates that China still has over 50 million Buddhists and 20 million Muslims. Not so surprising when we realise that a quarter of the world's population does after all live in China. In those terms the surviving Christian population – estimated by some Chinese church leaders at about 6 million – is a tiny drop in the Chinese ocean. But it still accounts for more Christians than there were in 1949, and the little flock is once again growing.

The British and Irish delegation is in China at the invitation of the Protestant China Christian Council – seven representatives of which, led by Bishop Ding, visited our own country last year, in September 1982. The purpose of the return visit is for the archbishop and his colleagues to see at first hand something of what is happening within the Chinese church and to build on the goodwill already established.

It will also give at least one member of the delegation – Dr Jack Weir, General Secretary of the Presbyterian Church in Ireland – an opportunity to return to the place where he was born. His father was a missionary and his first language was Chinese, though he claims he's forgotten most of it now.

Christianity used to be regarded by many Chinese as a foreign capitalist religion. It still is by many educated Chinese. Today, church leaders want to build a church with a Chinese face – a church governed, supported and nurtured by *Chinese*

Christians themselves. And Chinese Christians can be – indeed are – politically patriotic and progressive. This patriotism, they say, is recognised by the present communist leaders. About 1,000 churches are now said to have been reopened for Protestants and Anglicans, and 1 million copies of the Bible were due to be printed by the end of 1982, with many more this year.

The position of Catholics, however, is more fraught. The community is split between the Catholic Patriotic Association which can worship openly, and is in theory independent of Rome, and the underground Catholics who have to worship in secret. Recent attempts by the Vatican to re-establish former relationships have been rebuffed. A house church movement also exists – though estimates of its strength fluctuate wildly.

When Bishop Ding came to London last year, he gave an address at Lambeth Palace. It was not about Chinese socialism or the difficult years of the Cultural Revolution, but about resurrection. That was the word, he said, which was most descriptive of their experiences. Christians, he said, have tried so often to seal Jesus up in his tomb with big heavy stones. But the living Christ, he said, broke out of any man-made tomb, and Chinese Christians were now knowing the Risen Christ as if for the first time.

3 December 1983

Fortune Telling

Owing to the rude hastiness of air travel, I spent most of Christmas feeling that half of me was still in Hong Kong. Memories of sunshine sparkling on the sea and skyscrapers of that oriental harbour brought a whole new dimension to the word 'disorientated'. Although Hong Kong itself is superficially littered with Christmas decorations and the government has arranged for Christmas carols to be piped into tube stations as background music, the shortest walk around the streets shows that the dominant religion is not Christianity but Chinese traditional folk religion. If you keep a sharp eye open, you can see tiny shrines everywhere, even at the side of a newspaper vendor's stand. Though the *British* happen to *rule* Hong Kong, it is very definitely a *Chinese* society. It is also very definitely a capitalist one!

I was in Hong Kong to gather material for a documentary about how the different religious groups there are preparing for 1997 – that telling date when the British lease finally runs out, and the colony reverts to communist China.

I don't want to pre-empt that radio programme here, but one thing was clear. Although there's a lot of talk on the lines of 'our faith will carry us through', from Buddhists, Taoists and Christians, there *is* a great deal of anxiety. When the Archbishop of Canterbury arrived in Hong Kong after spending two and a half weeks in China, he was surrounded by cameramen and journalists who wanted to hear not about the Chinese church, but about whether he had discussed the future of Hong Kong with any of his Chinese hosts. His statement that the subject had not been raised at any of his conversations with Chinese leaders infuriated one Hong Kong Christian I spoke with. This man found it practically inconceivable that the archbishop had sidestepped the one subject that so profoundly affected the future of himself and his friends. He spoke of the archbishop's diplomatic silence as if it were a personal betrayal.

But others were less forthcoming about their fears for the future.

We noticed some busy burying of heads in the sand, including a Micawberish belief that everything would turn out all right in the end. Not surprisingly, some of those most opposed to communism were reluctant to say so publicly. The Chinese Communist Party is renowned in Asia for having a long memory. And for the moment a fair number of people are waiting to see what happens.

A clear stand, however, was taken by the spokesman for the Roman Catholic bishop in Hong Kong. He had no truck with any notion of a Hong Kong Catholic Church proclaiming itself independent of the Vatican. He said the Roman Catholic

Church in Hong Kong would never agree to work with the officially approved Chinese Catholic Patriotic Association.

But the issue that will affect the lives of most Hong Kongers will be the Chinese government's attitude to the traditional Chinese folk religion, a mixture of Buddhism, Taoism, Confucianism and popular fortune-telling and divination, which is at present frowned upon and discouraged by the communist-led government in Peking. Whereas the Chinese government officially accepts Islam, Buddhism, Christianity and, to a lesser extent, Taoism as 'religions', it regards folk religion as 'superstition'.

While in Hong Kong I visited a community temple where this folk religion is thriving. Before one of the shrines, people were kneeling in a courtyard, praying and shaking bamboo vases containing several dozen numbered sticks. One of the women there was praying to the God to heal her sore eye. Eventually one of the sticks was shaken out. She went to a dispensary at the other side of the courtyard and asked for the prescription that tallied with the number on the stick. Next to that dispensary was another counter where people were getting medicines prescribed, this time by a doctor. I asked the woman why she did not go to the doctor. She said she'd done so in the past, but it was the *God's* prescriptions that made her feel better.

It remains to be seen whether, after 1997, she and hundreds of thousands like her will be able to carry on this healing by faith, ancestor worship, fortune-telling and so on. Certainly the communists are finding it a much tougher job than they reckoned to put an end to such practices in China.

31 December 1983

A Glimpse of Heaven

Half-way up the Mount of Olives in Jerusalem stands an exquisite church, crowned with golden onion-shaped domes, in a garden of olive, lemon and cypress trees. It's the church of St Mary Magdalen, run by a community of about twenty nuns of the Russian Orthodox Church in exile. Although they're known affectionately in Jerusalem as White Russians, a number of the nuns these days are Arabs, and – typical of the Holy Land's paradoxes – for many years the community was led by a Scotswoman. So they speak a mixture of English, French, Arabic and Russian, and day in, day out, within their walled garden they sing the holy liturgy.

At midnight at the break of Easter Day, they began their celebrations for the Risen Christ and for me it was one of the most wonderful services I have ever attended. I caught a glimpse of an ancient tradition of worship, which to us in the west has almost entirely been lost.

I arrived about twenty mintes before the service itself began, though the preparations had been going on for weeks. Since the beginning of Lent, the nuns had been fasting – no meat, fish, eggs, butter or cheese. Sister Nadia, indeed, who leads the singers with perfect pitch, had lost nearly a stone in weight. On Holy Saturday night, the last touches were being made. One nun was rolling out the carpet, another was perched up a 20-foot step-ladder lighting the candles on a high ring chandelier. Others were lighting hundreds of candles around the sanctuary. At three minutes to midnight they were ready, holding icons and standing quietly before the screen in front of the altar.

At midnight the clock rang and the sound of men's voices quietly singing drifted across from near the altar. The sound rose and chinks of light began to glow from the sanctuary. Then the voices swelled up, the sanctuary doors were thrown open and the light filled the church. The bells chimed joyfully outside. Easter had come. Christ was risen. Over the next four hours, they celebrated the eucharist, declared again and again to each other that Christ was risen, and greeted each other with the kiss of peace. At half-past two I left for my bed, for a couple of hours' sleep before moving on to record another service elsewhere at six.

I once heard an Anglican scholar in England quip that whereas the chief preoccupation of the Eastern Orthodox worshipper is to find God, the chief preoccupation of the Anglican worshipper is to find the right page.

His remark of course unfairly compared the best of orthodox worship with the worst of the Anglican, and in our literal age, the mystical approach of orthodox worship can sometimes seem exclusive, repetitive, over-elaborate. But what struck me most about the service in Jerusalem was the way it radiated joy and harmony. Here were people who felt that to worship God was a foretaste of heaven and that to do so with others they loved was a pleasure not to be rushed through, but to be savoured and repeated. 'Christ is risen,' said the priests again and again, before processing through the congregation. 'He is risen indeed,' we replied, in our various languages.

It's an understatement to say that the Russian Orthodox Church in exile is not on the whole very interested in ecumenical talks with other branches of the Christian church. And it has fundamental political and other differences with the so-called Red Russians in Jerusalem – those members of the Russian Orthodox Church who accept the authority of the present Moscow patriarchate and have a rival church up the road. But to me the worship of the White Russians was marvellous for its coherence and commitment. And the tea and welcome provided by one of the nuns to a colleague of mine suffering from back pain was a reminder that homeliness and prayer, humour and reverence can exist very well together.

28 April 1984

Geneva Hotspot

If you sit quietly for half an hour one morning in a corner of the cool entrance hall of the headquarters of the World Council of Churches here in Geneva, as I did yesterday, you can see the ecclesiastical equivalent of the United Nations. Over by the bookshop is a woman minister in colourful dress from one of the Reformed churches in Africa. Rushing by with a bulging briefcase is a Russian Orthodox archbishop, complete with beard, gold cross, and a black high hat, his long black gown swishing the floor. Wandering towards the sunlit trees may be a more familiar figure, Dr John Habgood, the Archbishop of York, who only five days ago was watching the burning of York Minster. He's now dressed not in episcopal purple, but in shirt sleeves for the summer heat. They are all members of the council's 150-strong central committee, which is meeting in Geneva this week to plan the priorities of the next few years of the council's life and work.

One of the central committee's key jobs this time has been to confirm the choice of a new General Secretary. The man picked by the international administrations committee, after months of ecclesiastical in-fighting, is Dr Emilio Castro. He's a Methodist minister who was born fifty-seven years ago in a working-class Roman Catholic family in Uruguay, the sixth of nine children. For nine years he directed the council's commission on evangelism and mission. He replaces Dr Philip Potter, from the Caribbean, who retires in a few months' time after twelve controversial years as the council's General Secretary and chief executive.

Dr Castro will certainly need a deal of stamina and energy to survive what most people are agreed is an impossible job. His main role, I suppose, is to pontificate (from the Latin *pons*, a bridge). For he has to be a bridge-builder between Christians whose history over 2,000 years has created chasms of differences.

The World Council of Churches was originally founded in 1948. Its aim? To work towards the unity of the world-wide Christian church. It describes itself as a 'fellowship of churches which confess the Lord Jesus Christ as God and Saviour according to the Scriptures'. Today it has grown to a fellowship of some 300 Protestant, Anglican and Orthodox, but not Roman Catholic, churches from more than 100 countries. And certainly Dr Potter sees it as a miracle of grace that during these last thirty-six years they've been increasingly drawn together despite the preceding long centuries of division, isolation and rivalry.

But there are still great problems. I've catalogued elsewhere the growing strength gained from the shared worship – illustrated best at the huge assembly in Vancouver last summer – and the achievements in theological discussions. But I've catalogued too the tensions that have arisen from the left-wing stance of many of the social and political statements the council has made in recent years. These statements have developed out of a Third World theology which sees the church as speaking for those who otherwise have no voice. Dr Castro, the new General Secretary, wants to wait until the end of the central committee meeting before commenting on his priorities for the next few years. But broadly he's in sympathy with what has gone before, though his style is likely to be less challenging than that of his predecessor. But he does seem more aware than Dr Potter that the council has a huge communications problem.

When I arrived, a pile of documents were waiting for me in a pigeon-hole. They were copies of speeches, press releases, reports of the work of units and subcommittees and so on. When I had waded through them, I knew – if nothing else – that the council was against sin and in favour of justice and peace. Let me give you one illustration of the style. This comes from a report on the so-called 'Vancouver mandate on theological diversity and coherence in the World Council'. This, in effect, encouraged Christians of different traditions to share with each other their experience of God. The Vancouver mandate proposed, the document said, 'the development of vital and coherent interrelationships in theological work and called for interaction between the diversity of theological approaches'. Who needs gobbledegook when you have language like that? If Dr Castro over the next ten years can get even one of the council's committees to say what they mean clearly and simply, he will have earned the gratitude not only of the entire press corps, but of Christians all over the world who believe that the world council may be worth listening to.

14 July 1984

First Aid

You wouldn't think that an organisation that upped its income by over 70 per cent in the last year would be facing anxieties about the future. But such anxieties will undoubtedly surface next week at the spring assembly of the British Council of Churches in Liverpool, when it debates the future direction of its best known division – Christian Aid. You may remember that last year Christian Aid's director, Dr Charles Elliott, resigned after only two years in the post. And over the last few months the public response to the Ethiopian famine has put new stresses and strains on the organisation. Whereas in the previous year, Christian Aid's income was just over £11 million, this year it's likely to end up nearer £20 million.

This surge of new income is by no means unique to Christian Aid. Other overseas aid agencies like the Save the Children Fund, OXFAM and War on Want have similarly had to adjust to new levels of organisation and spending. But in Christian Aid's case, it has brought to a head questions about aims and priorities. These have been hotly debated inside the organisation for some time, but have not properly surfaced publicly in the assembly which sponsors the charity and appoints its governing board. In effect, Christian Aid's acting director, Martin Bax, is now asking the assembly to have its say. And to sharpen things up, he's prepared a commendably honest, though necessarily brief, background paper. It's fascinating reading for anyone who cares about the future of Christian Aid and its aims. The report starts by mapping out various changing international factors which are affecting Christian Aid's work. These are the collapse of the economies of a number of African countries, worsened by adverse weather conditions like the drought in Ethiopia. Then there's the increasing political polarisation in some parts of the world, accompanied all too often by violations of human rights. Then says Mr Bax there is diminishing hope that anything will emerge from efforts by UN and European organisations to improve international trading relations for the benefit of poorer countries.

These pressures, one might think, might be enough, but interchurch agencies have extra challenges on top. Christian Aid has always tried to channel most of its development work and relief aid through church-related organisations overseas. This implies consulting widely with different partner churches. But what happens if all this consultation slows things down and makes operations less efficient?

The worsening international situation and the plight of the starving has had the effect of spurring some Christian Aid supporters into making new demands on the agency. Some want the charity to establish a higher public profile. More and more church groups are ringing up or writing in for information and sending requests for speakers. Yet Christian Aid has far fewer staff than, say, OXFAM. Whereas OXFAM's income is double that of Christian Aid, OXFAM has more than four times as many full-time staff. Some supporters, too, want to know more clearly what their particular gift is being spent on. In response to that sort of pressure, some charities have launched Adopt-a-Granny or Adopt-a-Child schemes, where the gift becomes more personal. But Christian Aid has always staunchly resisted that, arguing that such giving can cause tensions where, say, one child in a family suddenly becomes relatively wealthy and another child may not. To follow donations through in other ways can, they say, be wildly uneconomic.

It's in response to these and other considerations that Christian Aid is now reorganising itself. But despite these moves, important decisions on various matters of *principle* also need to be taken in the near future.

And these are what the British Council of Churches Assembly will discuss next week. For instance, where should Christian Aid concentrate its efforts – in areas where the people are poorest or most repressed? Should it concentrate its aid on some countries and reduce its links with others? How important is it to spend money primarily through *church* partners? Then there's the educational side. How important is Christian Aid's work in educating churchgoers about the need for changes in international trading relationships? Or is this now a waste of time given the lack of government response to the international development questions raised in the Brandt report? The assembly is unlikely to give any clear-cut answers to these fundamental and incredibly complicated questions. But the assembly will know better what the difficulties are, and may even encourage those who struggle with these dilemmas every day of their working lives.

23 March 1985

Moscow in May

One of the fascinations of driving round the wide open streets of Moscow, past the modern blocks of flats and the state buildings in the socialist Gothic style so admired by Stalin, is seeing Soviet advertisements. Much more noble in sentiment than those in the west. 'All hail', reads one great placard, 'all hail to the peaceful Leninist foreign policy of the USSR.'

Certainly for the last few years, the Kremlin has done a great deal to assure its own citizens that its foreign policy aims are peaceful, and that warmongering and aggression are features of western policy. You can imagine the effect President Reagan's denunciation this week of the SALT Two arms limitation treaty is having on such Soviet citizens. It feels like confirmation of what their government is regularly telling them. To try to persuade even Soviet Christians that most people in the west are as frightened of *Soviet* military might as they are of *American* weapons is an uphill struggle. Yet that has been one of the messages of the delegation of British and Irish Christians who have just returned from an eleven-day visit to the Soviet churches.

The aim of the delegation was to repay a visit by Soviet Christians to Britain and Ireland three years ago, and to get to know more about the life and worship of the church in the USSR.

Overall, things are extremely complex – and not least the relationship of the Russian Orthodox Church – the old national church – to the state. Imagine a church where the state has a veto on all top appointments. Where the main governing body of the church cannot meet without the permission of the secular powers. A church that has fewer churches open than it did fifteen years ago. These are substantial, unacceptable restrictions, you might feel. Yet what I have described applies not only to the Russian Orthodox Church, but also the Church of England.

The key difference between state influence in the USSR and the United Kingdom is that whereas *British* governments are still basically sympathetic or neutral to the church (despite minor or even major irritations), the policy of the *Soviet* state is dictated by a party whose philosophy is essentially hostile to it.

Well, given the differences, how free *are* the Soviet churches? It it clear that no one would be appointed bishop in the Russian Orthodox Church if the state felt it couldn't work with him. The constitution guarantees freedom of belief, but freedom of action or speech is another thing altogether.

For instance, Christians who refuse to register their groups with the state are charged with breaking the law. Religious groups are forbidden to produce or distribute religious literature without official permission. They may not use funds for any charitable or social work apart from donations to Soviet peace committees. Nor may they legally organise youth clubs, Sunday schools, wives groups or mothers unions. But in practice, some ways are found round some of these restrictions. For instance, some collective religious education is being given. There are reports in some areas of atheist officials repressively going beyond the law. In other places a liberal blind eye is being turned to some of the law's restrictions. The Russian Orthodox Church has several monasteries and five academies and seminaries with something like 2,000 students at the moment. In parts of the east of the USSR you can go for hundreds of miles without seeing a church, but in Moscow there are about forty open Russian Orthodox churches. In Armenia I was told unofficially baptisms are as high as 80 per cent. In a television broadcast last week, even a Soviet commentator admitted that in rural areas as many as 17 per cent of people could still be believers.

The picture that emerges is of a growing church, marvellously rich and intense worship, flourishing despite restrictions. In Moscow, for instance, at the Russian Orthodox Cathedral, over 1,000 Christians stood packed in before the magnificent gold screen hung with icons, the candles flickering nearby, smelling the incense and listening to the beautiful singing that filled the church.

It's a sobering thought that over sixty years of atheist propaganda has arguably had less effect in diminishing religious faith than sixty years of religious complacency at home.

31 May 1986

One-Thumb White Boss

One hundred years ago last Tuesday, on 29 October 1885, a Sussex bishop was speared to death by African tribesmen. He was the first of forty-one Anglican and Roman Catholic martyrs who died in the months following, in the part of Africa now known as Uganda. Bishop James Hannington was known to some as 'One-Thumb White Boss' because of a boyhood accident with a bomb made to destroy a wasps' nest.

In October 1885 he was on his way to Buganda, one of the four states which now make up Uganda, as the first bishop of East Equatorial Africa. He died at the hands of a chief loyal to the then ruler of the state.

But Christianity did establish itself. Since then, it has been inextricably woven into the political and social life of the country. Only recently the Roman Catholic Cardinal Emmanuel Nsubuga was trying to achieve reconciliation between the government of General Tito Okello, who ousted President Obote in a coup in July, and the guerrillas led by another group which holds large parts of the country. Today's political instability and tribal rivalry are one of the continuing problems aggravated by the rule in the 1970s of Idi Amin.

The story of Christianity in Uganda began just a few years before Hannington's murder, with the arrival of the explorer H. M. Stanley at the court of the ruler of Buganda, known as the Kabaka. The Kabaka, Mutesa I, was interested in the political support Stanley's white people could give him against Muslim Arab traders in the north. In 1875 the *Daily Telegraph* printed a letter from Stanley appealing for funds for missionaries. And in 1877 the first two Anglican missionaries arrived. They brought with them no strategy, except to evangelise. This attitude rather puzzled the Kabaka, as it seemed to offer little of practical value – like firearms, for instance.

When the Anglicans were followed a couple of years later by

Roman Catholic missionaries, who proceeded to tell the Africans that they had not so far heard *true* Christianity, Mutesa and his court became confused. Some of the future leaders of the Kabaka's court were converted. But when Mutesa died and was succeeded by his son Mwanga, renowned for his cruelty, persecutions began. Many of the martyrs were burnt alive.

This unhappy period was followed by political and religious wars. First the Protestants and Catholics joined forces against the Muslims, then they turned against each other. It was an unedifying period, when bitterness burnt deep. There are still traces of the old rivalries in Anglican-Catholic relationships in Uganda today. Eventually the British declared the country a protectorate, and the Protestants gained political ascendancy, although they were fewer.

As usual the church brought with it schools, hospitals and western ideas. Before and since independence in 1962, local African leadership has been developed, with now less and less foreign influence. During Amin's period the church, like so many other sections of Ugandan society, came under intense pressure. In 1977, the Anglican Archbishop Luwum was murdered and others too have died since. The thread of martyrdom has been a constant theme in the history of the Ugandan church.

Earlier this year, a group of visitors from Anglican provinces around the world spent some time in Uganda for a consultation known as Partners in Mission. Their reports reflected the great differences in the dioceses – ranging from the nomadic tribes of the Karamoja to the industrial city of Jinja. But they all had a common message: the need for more and better trained clergy, better youth training, and programmes to support Christian marriage at a time when even some church people are lapsing into polygamy. By far the most sensitive subject was the whole question of human rights and whether the churches should speak up more strongly against the murders and other brutalities being committed around the country – in some places by government troops.

The Anglican bishops have recently sent a memo to the

ruling military council, suggesting the suspension of political parties for a year before elections are held. They have also called for a round-the-table peace conference, a revision of the constitution and a carefully planned programme to resettle displaced people and those returning to their homes. They've expressed alarm at the victimisation of individuals on the basis of their politics, religious beliefs or tribe.

With all that on their minds, it's not surprising that the bishops have postponed the centenary ceremonies marking Bishop Hannington's martyrdom.

2 November 1985

Heat and Dust

Heat and dust and flies and crowds. Some of the signs that have greeted the Pope at the start of his ten-day visit to India. India, it seems, is the religious place of the moment. The Archbishop of Canterbury arrives for a visit later this month (he and the Pope will be meeting briefly). And yesterday a group of forty British Jews left London for Bombay at the beginning of a fortnight's tour of places of general and Jewish interest – schools and synagogues and the like.

Hinduism – in its myriad and fascinating forms – is so obviously the dominant religion in India that it may at first seem strange that the papal visit has so distressed some Hindus. Christianity after all accounts for only 3 per cent of India's 750 million. But demos and worse are threatened. The other day the Archbishop of Madras received an anonymous telegram threatening assassination of the Pope. But then, as Vatican officials wearily say, such threats are 'normal' for a papal visit.

The anxiety seems to be that the Pope will come along and convert many Hindus to Christianity. A number of converts have been made lately among some of the hill villagers in the north-east, who were formerly animist. And some members of the lowest Hindu caste – the untouchables – are still particularly susceptible to Christian conversion. After all, if you are re-garded as being on the lowest rung of the human ladder, Christian teachings of equality in the sight of the creator must sound specially appealing. But such conversions still can spark off difficulties. In Andhra Pradesh last July [1985] six people died during a dispute between a community of Christian con-verts and Hindu villagers of a higher caste.

The Pope will have to walk warily.

Well, he has told the Indian ambassador to the Holy See that he hopes the visit will make clear his 'heartfelt respect for India's spiritual traditions'. As part of his preparations he has been studying eastern religion and philosophy with an Indian Jesuit priest. He has been learning phrases from some of India's fifteen official languages.

But what will he say? Well, he's likely to repeat his appeals for a better economic deal for Third World countries. He will call for harmony between different religious groups and for united efforts to work for social justice, *together*.

Christians in India have on the whole a good record in practical matters. Catholics, for instance, run over a quarter of India's schools and over a fifth of its hospitals. But in secular terms the tricky subject is that of birth control. In a country where the government has conducted massive campaigns to promote artificial birth control, the Pope's views will not be exactly welcome to many government officials. True, many would agree with him and his bishops that the best answer to combat poverty is by trade and development. But in the mean time, they argue, population control is needed as well.

Within the Roman Catholic Church itself, the most sensitive subject in India is probably the question 'How far should the church adapt its traditions to local culture?' That problem exercises bishops all over the world. Once seminary students from India and Africa and the Philippines and so on were nearly all taught in Latin and the church modelled its worship and administration on Rome. The Second Vatican Council, twen-ty-five years ago, changed that, by authorising adaptations to local culture. Some Indian gestures have been adopted – as when you join your hands together to greet someone. Some priests wear yellow shawls and have introduced dance into the worship. But there are still arguments about how far this can go.

It's complicated in India by the fact that historically there are different church traditions. The earliest claims go right back to the first century. Local legend has it that St Thomas – doubting Thomas – came to South India to found the church. The descendants of these early Christians follow ancient Indian Christian rites.

But in the sixteenth century, missionaries brought the Roman form of Christianity to India. A compromise was worked out eventually whereby the ancient native oriental church was restricted to Kerala in the south and the rest of India was put under the jurisdiction of the Roman church. This agreement is resented by some of the Kerala clergy, who would like their own patriarch and permission to establish bishops in other parts of India.

One of the jobs of the Pope in the next fortnight will be to try to resolve this delicate problem. The theme of the visit is after all peace and unity.

1 February 1986

There Is a Green Hill . . .

Just a mile or so away from the teeming, dirty, dusty centre of Uganda's capital Kampala, are two green hills. To get there from the centre of the town, you climb into a packed local mini-bus, which will jolt its way round the worst pot-holes, past the rubbish dumps and the half-empty shops with bullet holes in the windows and weeds growing from the roofs. On each hill is a cathedral. One, Rubaga, is for the Roman Catholics. The other is for the Anglicans. The name of the Anglican hill is Namirembe, which means peace. Yet the Bishop of Namirembe, a dear man who wears his bishop's hat like a scout cap, estimates that in his diocese over the last five years, up to half a million people have been killed.

British television has shown pictures of groups of human skulls, displayed at roadsides, as evidence of killing. But I was unprepared for the sight of places where the ground was littered with human bones. I saw human wrists still manacled together with wire and steel, with pathetic rags of blood-stained, civilian clothing attached. Some skulls had been shattered by a blunt instrument, others sliced by an axe. Some had burn marks on the top of their head – thought to have been caused by torture, red-hot drips of molten plastic.

The local people say that the vast majority of these killings were reprisals by army soldiers against villagers accused of supporting guerrillas who were operating from the area. In the early months of this year, those underpaid, underfed, ill-disciplined soldiers were finally put to flight, and the guerrillas of the National Resistance Army under Yoweri Museveni took control of the government of Uganda.

The task of both church and government now is to try to rebuild the moral and physical fabric of the country. In some areas farming has been neglected for years. The narrow dirt-track roads have become overgrown. There are burnt-out houses, abandoned churches with their roofs plundered long ago, homes with bullet marks splattering the walls. In other places the civil war had different effects. In parts of the north, political instability led to extensive looting. Bad roads, language difficulties and inadequate communication hinder any sense of national identity. Uganda sometimes feels like several different countries, rather than one.

Then there is the problem of economic collapse. In the past few years the value of the Ugandan shilling has plummeted. The second time I changed money in Uganda, to hire a car, I needed so many Ugandan notes that they were delivered to me in a shoe box. A Church of Ugandan pastor in the Namirembe diocese has to buy only four large bunches of green bananas in the market to spend his month's salary. Not surprisingly, most people are trying to grow food of their own, or to earn extra income on the side. The black market is flourishing, so is bribery. In the south-west, economic survival is helped by smuggling in basic commodities like soap, matches and salt from the neighbouring country of Rwanda.

All this creates many difficulties for the church. I heard a number of sermons against corruption and financial misdealing. But pastors and priests are well aware how poor are some members of their congregations. In Gulu in the north, I was told by a Roman Catholic nun that the government had not paid teachers' wages since December, and that the government hospitals in general were also in bad shape. The churches' contribution to schooling and job training and the mission hospitals is now even more important than before.

Wherever I went, Ugandan Christians sent warm greetings to the church in Britain. When asked how the British churches could best help them, they said, 'Pray for us.' When pressed, they said they needed things like hoes and seeds, medical supplies and books and scholarships to Britain to help them train future church leaders.

Uganda is a green and fertile country. Now is the growing season. All over the country people are beginning again, planting what they can where they can. They hope desperately, this time, the seed will not fall among thorns.

10 May 1986

Soviet Icons

London this week has been boiling and packed with foreign visitors – most of them, it seems, buying up the remaining bargains in the sales. But one visitor who had no time for the simmering pavements of Oxford Street was the Soviet Foreign Minister, Mr Eduard Shevardnadze, who's been having talks with the Prime Minister and the Foreign Secretary. At a news conference on Wednesday he revealed that the talks between the United States and the Soviet Union on banning nuclear tests are to begin in Geneva later this month. But whereas the Soviet emphasis is likely to be on the problem of achieving a more comprehensive ban on nuclear tests, like the US one this week in Nevada, the Americans are chiefly concerned with ways of verifying that the existing limiting agreements are being enforced. The difficulties of verification point up the old problem of the gap between the ideal and the real.

Very soon the British Council of Churches is to publish an account of the recent visit of a delegation of nineteen British and Irish Christians to churches in the Soviet Union. And at one place the account talks about this very thing – the gap between the ideal and the real, and the characteristic tendency of Soviet life, both religious and secular, to portray and emphasise the ideal. You have only to spend a little time watching Soviet TV or reading Soviet newspapers to see the tremendous emphasis on good news. Stories of farms and industries doing well, exceeding their expected output and efficiency. These are models of excellence, of the ideal. To many Soviet broadcasters and journalists the western habit of reporting bad news, often stories of failure which not only do not reflect the ideal, but do not even reflect the norm, is seen as a negative, even bizarre way of looking at things.

For me all this was put into fascinating perspective by a member of the British church delegation. He said that the visit had confirmed for him the need for westerners to understand iconography – that is, the portrait of the ideal – and how it has penetrated the whole of Soviet life, both secular and religious. Every Soviet church is an attempt to depict heaven. It does not merely proclaim the risen Christ. It *is* the good news of the risen life. As you walk into a Russian Orthodox church, you see, before the altar, a huge screen hung with icons. These are idealised portraits of the saints. In their making, they are not so much painted as prayed. The icon painter paints a little and prays. The portraits are in themselves an act of worship and meditation. And the fruits of this worship are revealed in the golden aura of peace which glows from them. For Russian Christians these represent true reality. What the member of the

British church delegation was saying was that in the Soviet Union, church and state were so interwoven for centuries that a similar iconography still penetrates even secular life. Interestingly there are some signs of iconoclasm – that is, destruction of such icons – in the Gorbachov era. For instance, corruption in Soviet life, drug-taking, alcoholism, embezzlement and so on are now much more in the open. Yet it's still unacceptable to suggest publicly that the Communist Party might be less than the perfect interpretation of Leninist socialism. Drunken priests and party officials there may be, but both the party and the church reject a less than infallible public image. To a modern western way of thinking this is difficult to cope with.

In the Soviet Union gaps between the ideal and the real are sometimes painful to observe. For instance, the British church delegation was told that Baptist churches are opening every year. But according to Keston College, more are closing down. Keston also reports that although many churches are allowed by the state to register officially, thousands of church groups have not been given the necessary permission. This is not mentioned publicly in the Soviet Union.

The trouble with a society which is always presenting public ideals is that it tends to create structures where realistic dialogue – say, between church and state – is hard to achieve. You can end up with blocs living in closed worlds with no real communication. It's a reminder of the difficulties that will face the arms negotiators in Geneva.

19 July 1986

Black Hat

I had a letter this week from Nicaragua. A country not well known here, though its name has been often enough in news stories lately. The circular letter arrived only a day or two after the news that President Reagan was asking Congress for an extra $100 million to fund the Contras, who want to overthrow the Sandinista government. And it put things in rather a different perspective.

The letter came from Father John Medcalf, the only English priest in Nicaragua. Dated 12 December 1986, it describes a series of visits he made on horseback to 'comarcas' or regions in what was once tropical rain forest. A typical comarca would have thirty or forty wooden farmsteads, spread out over the hills, linked by a muddy track. Usually the only public building would be the Catholic chapel, though sometimes there's an evangelical chapel as well. Fortunately, he says, he's not yet met the Contras, though they're never far away. As he rides beside his local guide, there's plenty to help him forget the agony of war. The very names of the comarcas are suggestive enough – Painted Rock, Black Hat, Conformity, Edible Iguana and Wild Bee Hive.

On 13 November 1986, in the comarca of Las Pavas (which means 'turkey hens') he was given a great welcome by the local lay preacher and leader, known as the delegate of the Word of God. Forty-five year old Zacarias Garzon had persuaded almost every family to attend the twenty-four-hour mission Father Medcalf was to direct in the chapel. The chapel had also been used as a school until the Contras abducted the teacher.

He introduced Medcalf, cheerfully reminding his fellow farmers that most of the Englishmen who'd visited the Caribbean in the past had been pirates looking for Spanish gold. In his reply Father Medcalf suggested that turkeys, Central America's gift to the world, had brought more pleasures to Britain than Spanish gold. There followed many hours of baptisms, weddings, first communions and question-and-answer sermons. Long after sundown, they were still talking. By then the subject had got round to the exact meaning of the commandment 'Thou shalt not kill'. Zacarias Garzon seemed content to direct the debate without proffering an opinion of his own.

Father Medcalf wonders if he had some kind of premonition, for three weeks later, on 2 December, the Contras dragged Garzon from his hut and slit his throat in the nearby forest. Father Medcalf says he doesn't know why. Although one of

Garzon's nephews works for the Ministry of Agriculture, Zacarias was not known to be a Sandinista supporter, and indeed in this part of Nicaragua, which my correspondent describes as a political no-man's land, nobody declares their political allegiance except in the secrecy of the confessional. Perhaps, he wonders, the Contras are afraid of strong leadership.

This is just one death out of many. So much has been more dramatic; bridges blown up, teachers raped and abducted, border villages strafed by fighter planes provided by the United States. In Father Medcalf's own parish, he goes on, villagers are opening up their homes to war orphans, even though they could be made targets of Contra reprisals for doing so.

But for him, he writes, Zacarias is more real than all this – the delegate of the Word of God who welcomed him only a few weeks before Christmas.

10 January 1987

Tears and Tear-Gas

Yesterday, police in Chile used tear-gas, water cannon and shotguns against left-wing protesters criticising the government at an outdoor Mass led by the Pope.

Priests came down from the platform to try to quell the turmoil. Meanwhile tear-gas drifted upwards, affecting some of the bishops with the Pope. It was the most violent outburst so far during the Pope's six-day visit – and yet another sign of the country's tensions. Already in the last few days, the visit has been marked by a series of telling incidents.

The Pope on the plane wandering down to the reporters' end and referring to what he described as the 'present dictatorial' political system in Chile. Then at the airport the passionate justification of military rule by President Pinochet, as a defence against what he sees as communist conspiracy. Then the Pope at the church human rights office in Santiago, being presented with a book containing the pictures of over 700 prisoners who have disappeared. 'I carry the disappeared prisoners in my heart,' he said.

Close to one service already this week, groups of young people have protested against the government and been chased by riot police. Several police were hurt by flying stones and bottles.

In the poor area of the city, the Pope sat on a raised platform before thousands of people. A housewife listed some of the problems of keeping a family together there – the husband out of work, or on slave wages if he is lucky enough to get a job, lack of medical facilities, and a shortage of teachers in slum schools. 'We live in anxiety,' she said. 'We don't want violence. We just want to live in dignity without dictatorship.'

Then there was the picture, back at the presidential palace, of the Pope and General Pinochet, praying together, kneeling on red cushions inside a small chapel. And perhaps the most telling image of all – the Pope addressing more than 80,000 young people, at an open-air Mass in Santiago's national football stadium. This was the same infamous stadium to which thousands of the government's political opponents were brought after the coup in 1973. Some were tortured. It's said that the wall against which some were shot was removed during the preparations for the Pope's visit.

Throughout this week the Pope has urged the return of democracy, but as he has said, with a smile, he is not the evangeliser of democracy. He is the evangeliser of the gospel.

It's in this context that he's appealed repeatedly against violence, and for reconciliation with justice.

At the service yesterday, he responded to the turmoil by continuing with the Mass and saying in his sermon that violence was neither Christian nor evangelical. Nor was it, he said, the way to solve real difficulties of individuals or peoples. Christianity, he went on, excluded hate, class struggles and reprisals.

Some of those who feel most passionately against the regime find it hard to understand how the Pope can pray and shake hands with the President, and kiss the grandchildren of the government's leaders, while at the same time criticising violence from all quarters in his speeches. Critics see such actions as providing symbolic support to the government.

But what the Pope is desperately trying to do is to encourage real dialogue and to avoid further polarising the country's politics. He wants to draw out the best from each side, and so respond to the vision he brings. Behind it is the Christian conviction that every single individual matters, and that each person – their politics or their past – can be changed. For to the Pope, change is at the heart of the gospel.

3 April 1987

Partners in Crime

Some time ago a couple of administrators from a western aid agency visited a diocese in Pakistan. They travelled around the villages seeing various development projects that were under way and afterwards returned to the bishop's house to talk about how they could help. After a while, the bishop said, 'Let me put one question to you. How can we, a tiny church in a Muslim society, most of whose members are economically poor, help your churches in the west?' There was a long pause. There was no answer.

That story was told me this week in the closing stages of the recent World Council of Churches conference on interchurch aid and refugees, which has been meeting in Larnaca, Cyprus. And it illustrates the strange relationship that exists between some of the different parts of the international church. The Bible teaches Christians that all men and women are made in the image of God and that all Christians together are children of God. How is it then that members of western churches all too often operate on the unspoken – and sometimes unrecognised – assumption that what *they* have to give is specially important? In a way that question highlights the immense problems in developing a real sense of partnership between the international churches. By half-way through the conference some frustra-

tions had been expressed by some of the Third World partici-
pants who felt that churches from the richer north still often
discount their experience – both spiritual and economic. It was
at this point that contributions by observers from other faiths
threw new shafts of light.

First of all, the Jewish observer who directs a Jewish aid
agency gently suggested to the conference members that they
might do better working out what could in fact be achieved
practically, rather than talking dreams about new international
economic orders.

As for the Buddhist, he took up an idea that had been much
discussed – the parable of the Good Samaritan, who helps the
man on the road to Jericho who has been beaten up and robbed,
while the priest and the Levite pass by on the other side. He
suggested that Christians were often well intentioned but sometimes seemed to lack a critical self-awareness. You may be the
Good Samaritan, he said, but you may also be the robber, or the
priest, or the Levite.

But what I found most helpful was the contribution from the
Hindu, Mr Rada Krishna, from the Gandhi Foundation in
India. He explored the meaning of the conference theme of
diakonia, the Greek word for service. It included certainly, he
said, ideas of justice and love, compassion, mercy and sharing.
But it was more than all those together. It meant, he said, our
own lives, our joy, our happiness. And it was this quest for joy
that was the beginning. It meant learning to see God in
everyone we meet and, through that, beginning to experience
the sense of being one family in one created universe.

And I suppose that was the heart of the question to the aid
administrators posed by the bishop in Pakistan. For if the
churches in the west think that it is only money and technology
that are worth sharing, we are in a very dark place indeed. For it
means we count as worthless things that cannot be assessed in
financial terms. Yet the church in Pakistan can surely offer us
things too. Its members know what it is to be poor and suffering. When they talk about Jesus they talk not about Christ
the King, but about the image of him prophesied in the book of

Jeremiah in the Bible, the suffering and rejected *servant*. And there are countless examples of sacrificial giving in the Third World. For instance, despite all their problems, the churches in Zambia and Ghana and the Martoma church in South India still managed to give money to relieve the suffering in Ethiopia. Africa harbours no less than half the world's refugees – 5 million people. Yet Africans have accepted people from neighbouring countries uprooted from their homes and even managed to share with them what little they have.

At these conferences, when you hear the pain and the stories of some of the international churches, the difficulties of becoming true servants to each other can feel overwhelming. Rada Krishna had something to say about that too. Don't get discouraged, he said. And he told the tale of a man on a long journey who, tired, enters a dark cottage to sleep. But when he awakes he finds a small lamp burning in the corner. It was another reminder that people of other faiths, as well as of the same faith, can sometimes be small lamps in dark places.

29 November 1986

Tallinn Tales

This time last week – Holy Saturday – it was a bright but icy day in Tallinn. A few light snowflakes fell on the cobbled streets of the old upper town, capital of the tiny Soviet republic of Estonia. But the sharpest cold blew in across the docks, from the Baltic Sea, still partly frozen. Some hardy workers, wrapped up in scarves and hats, were sweeping the streets, cleaning windows and the like. For this was the annual Subbotnik, the day shortly before Lenin's birthday, when Soviet citizens voluntarily donate a day's free labour to the country. But there was not a sign of any Easter festivity to be seen in the shops – not an egg, not a card, not a banner. Yet this town with less than half a million inhabitants has at least seventeen churches of several denominations, all still open for regular worship. Before 1940, when Estonia was still an independent country, the established church was the Lutheran Church. If you go into the oldest Lutheran building in town with its high Gothic arches and simple whitewashed walls, you can still see ornate coats of arms, and a comfortable windowed box with the best view and seats for the nobility. Now the church has a dusty declining air, though I was told the state has recently agreed to put money into the restoration of the building.

But other churches have a livelier spiritual atmosphere. Just up the road is St Olaf's Baptist church, where the American evangelist Billy Graham preached to several thousand in 1984. But the following year, three people from the church were charged with illegal trading in a video and cassette recording of the Graham service. The authorities say they were evading taxes, but many members of the church see the state's action as another way of restricting Christian evangelism. None of the three ended up in gaol, but the incident served as a warning.

Estonia was absorbed into (some say reunited with) the Soviet Union in 1940, and after the end of the war possibly as many as 60,000 Estonians were deported, and gradually Russians and other Soviet nationalities moved in. Today, nearly 30 per cent of the population is said to be of Russian origin. At Easter some of these attended a service at one of the four Russian Orthodox churches.

Last Saturday night just before midnight, I took part in worship at the small crowded cathedral in the upper town. A line of about eighty young naval cadets ringed the doorway, deterring from entering people who had not previously obtained a pass from the church. Some Christians insisted that the guard was there primarily to deter drunks who've caused trouble in the past. Certainly I saw no similar lines at three other services I attended elsewhere.

The long-term policy of the state regarding religion is clear – to allow freedom of worship to congregations accepted for registration, but to contain their activities so that gradually, stage by stage, religion will wither away, as socialist theory predicts.

In some places in the Soviet Union congregations *have* gradually dissolved, worn away by the surrounding sea of religious indifference and ignorance. But in other places – and in parts of Estonia – Christian life and experience and worship are isolated by Soviet policy. Some still believe they will one day be rejoined to the mainland. And they are waiting hopefully to see how far the new tides of '*glasnost*' and the rest will affect their particular landscape.

25 April 1987

3

DIVIDED
WE STAND

Bullets and Ballots

This week has been a week of ballots and bombs. We've had the two by-elections – both won, not very convincingly, by Labour, and the one in Peckham with such a low turn-out that over three people in every five couldn't be bothered to vote, or decided not to. There have been the miners, and British Leyland ballots on pay offers, and in Ulster, of course, the elections for the assembly that Mr Prior so hopes will set the province back on the road towards self-government. But the mood now is uncertain. Sinn Fein, the political wing of the IRA, has won five seats, which it says it will not take up. And once more the repellent trail of violence and counterviolence smears its way through the six counties.

It's part of my job to hear many sermons and speeches, and I've noticed that whenever church leaders talk about Ireland, the almost compulsory line 'violence never pays' slips in somewhere. It occurred to me again this week, what an arguable statement that is. Every terrorist knows that violence brings public attention to his or her cause, and the insult 'terrorist' can sometimes be gradually transformed into the phrase 'respected member of the government'. Look at Zimbabwe, Kenya, Israel and, most significantly, the Republic of Ireland. Would the republic have been created but for the violence? The argument of many church people when pressed on the subject is that such violence, it is true, has in *some* circumstances – though certainly not all – led to short-term political gain, but that in the long term, the effects are like poison – corrupting the individuals concerned. This was an argument put strongly by the Roman Catholic Bishop of Down and Connor this week. Speaking at the funeral of Mr Joseph Donegan, the Roman Catholic murdered by Protestant terrorists in a tit-for-tat killing, Bishop Cahal Daly gave a passionate exposition of the Christian response to violence. The only way to end violence, he said, was by forgiveness. Christ, he said, took the brutal force of violence upon his own defenceless body on the cross and he killed it non-violently in its tracks. He killed it by forgiving it. Just when the violence was doing to him its savage worst, he prayed 'Father, forgive them for they know not what they do.' Hatred, remarked Bishop Daly, merely recycles violence. It was, interestingly, an out-and-out pacifist sermon.

Bishop Cahal Daly was appointed Bishop of Down and Connor only recently, and it already begins to look as if his appointment could be an influential one in the community in the north. He has condemned terrorism on numerous occasions, and has made efforts to try to help the Roman Catholic community understand the point of view of the Protestants. One Presbyterian, for instance, told me he felt the bishop understood the trauma Protestants in Northern Ireland had undergone in recent years with the loss of some of their privileges – the right to self-government, and so on. To be quite frank, it looks as if any such bridges in understanding are certainly needed at the moment because communications between the churches are *not* at present in a happy state. Bedevilling everything is the issue of mixed marriages. In some areas, it's reported that some Roman Catholic priests are still asking the Protestant partner to sign a document agreeing that the children will be raised as Catholics – even though verbal consent is more common. A Roman Catholic directive on the subject has been delayed yet again, and in the mean time, tempers on the Anglican and Protestant side are getting more and more frayed. Meanwhile, the theological talks at Ballymascanlon between the Roman Catholic hierarchy and other church leaders, have been in abeyance over the past five years, though another meeting is planned for 1983. As for the Irish Council of Churches, that, like its British counterpart, still does not include Roman Catholics, and the members it *does* have are proving sometimes difficult to motivate. They are also reluctant to provide much cash. Some Presbyterians would even like their church to withdraw altogether. So I have to report that it looks as if the ecumenical movement – frail plant as it always was in Ireland – is wilting a bit. But it *is* still alive. The Corrymeela and Rostrevor communities, for instance, carry on their work of reconciliation, as do individuals, ministers, priests and lay people in various parishes. There's still a hope of spring.

30 October 1982

Apart at the Hinges

I discovered the other day, thanks to the *Church Times*, that the word 'cardinal' comes from a Latin word meaning 'a hinge'. Unfortunately there's no evidence whatever that the word 'bishop' stems from a Latin word for 'bracket'. That would indeed have put a whole new perspective on ecclesiastical gatherings. But it seems the word 'hinge' was probably a slang word for the advisers to the Bishop of Rome, who were his 'hingemen' or key clerics.

At the British Council of Churches spring assembly in Liverpool this week, there were no cardinals, but there were a lot of contemporary hingemen and women, from the Anglican, Protestant and Orthodox churches. All there, 200 of them, offering themselves to Jesus the carpenter as natural joints in the long process of reassembling the original piece of furniture – the universal church, which came apart some centuries ago.

Unfortunately I have to report that last week's meeting hardly moved things on very far. Moreover several members left the gathering feeling frustrated, even angry. What went wrong and what can be done?

First of all let me describe the scene – a university hall of residence surrounded by lawns, with the odd friendly duck waddling about. Inside are groups of church people – some of them well known, like the Archbishop of Canterbury, some leaders of church organisations like Christian Aid and the missionary societies, and some others who represent in fact not much more than themselves but are there because they volunteered.

Next the agenda. The first day was given to getting to know a bit about Liverpool itself. The afternoon was spent visiting different projects around the area – like the church shared by Anglicans and Roman Catholics, and the local law centre, to which the British Council of Churches gave £500 three years ago.

The next day, the real discussions began. A debate on priorities for Christian Aid went smoothly. Council members indicated they hoped Christian Aid would continue to channel as much of its development work as possible through church partners overseas. The council wants the agency to maintain this distinctive style of operating. But then a motion emerged criticising government slowness in responding to the crisis in Africa. One section of the resolution was quite technical, dealing with the World Bank's special fund for sub-Saharan Africa. Yet no briefing papers were initially provided and when the question was raised, no one could answer immediately how this resolution had got on to the agenda. The debate had to be halted for the executive to reorganise itself.

That afternoon came a debate on a so-called policy statement on east–west relations. This policy statement had never been requested by the council, and in fact turned out to be an extended essay drafted by one of the council's administrative staff, Canon Paul Oestreicher. The essay's approach to the two great power blocs of east and west was determinedly even-handed. For instance, it compared the 10,000 political prisoners in the Soviet Union denied human rights with well over 10,000 Americans killed every year by guns which their fellow

Americans had the right to carry. The essay suggested that when Christians put the Soviet Union in the dock, they should remember with humility how for centuries the church itself persecuted unloved minorities. A Roman Catholic observer at the assembly commented that while the Roman Catholic bishops in England and Wales welcomed a statement on human rights, they felt this particular statement did not take sufficient account of the sensitivities of the Roman Catholic Church in eastern Europe.

The assembly eventually insisted that the statement should be withdrawn for further revision. It also refused to endorse a resolution supporting the idea of a nuclear freeze. One speaker pointed out that in 1979 the assembly had already given its support to the phasing out of the British independent nuclear deterrent. The Archbishop of York complained that yet again, for the fourth time in six years, nuclear weapons appeared on the agenda.

It would be misleading to think a major row is brewing at the British Council of Churches. It is not. Church leaders are mostly anxious for everyone to get on well. And some members of the assembly are probably happy to be led in the direction the administrative staff would like them to take. But in private, there are growing grumbles and complaints. The staff at the council might reply that things would be easier if the member churches themselves had a clearer idea of where they wanted the council to go.

30 March 1985

Dutch Courage

On Thursday evening this week His Eminence the Roman Catholic Archbishop of Utrecht, primate of Holland, the newly created Cardinal Simonis, put on his bicycle clips and cycled through the old streets of the town, past the canals and the budding trees, to visit the Roman Catholic seminary where young men are training for the priesthood. He calls about twice a month, to share supper, to celebrate Mass and to say a few words. One reason for his special concern for the welfare of these seminarians is that Holland, like a number of other Roman Catholic countries, is desperately short of priests. Ordinations collapsed from 237 in 1965 down to only 21 in 1972. After the Second Vatican Council in the early 1960s, a wave of hundreds of priests resigned their posts – some to get married, some because the changes in the church led them to new pastures. The long-term effect of adjusting to that desertion from the traditional ranks of the celibate priesthood is just one of the problems facing the Dutch Roman Catholic church today as it prepares for a four-day pastoral visit to the Netherlands by Pope John Paul II. He arrives with his entourage next Saturday.

In Britain the controversy this week over whether Prince Charles should or should not have attended a Mass celebrated by the Pope has revealed some anti-papal feeling again. And not just among the followers of Dr Ian Paisley. Holland, too, has its group of fundamentalist Protestants still arguing in the language and concepts of the sixteenth and seventeenth centuries. But a visit to Holland this week – and I'm talking now from a studio in Hilversum – has reminded me of how most Dutch Christians would prefer these days no longer to dwell on the old rallying calls 'Reformed' or 'Calvinist' or 'Catholic', or on the bitterness such calls engendered in Dutch, as well as English, history. Over the last few years, many Dutch Christians have tried to share their different faiths and experiences in prayer, in discussion groups, in social activity and even at the communion table. The effects on the Roman Catholic Church in Holland have been remarkable. In place of the old Catholic certainties on moral issues, handed down by the church via the hierarchy, most Dutch Catholics prefer these days to trust to individual conscience – an emphasis that has strongly Protestant overtones.

As for Catholic theology in Holland – led by Professor Schillebeckx and others – *that* has been voraciously exploring the

Bible in the light of recent biblical scholarship and testing Catholic dogma against it. The result has been a frank questioning of traditional Catholic teaching on the role of women in the church, the celibacy of the priesthood, the power of the Pope and so on. When professional pastoral lay workers began to take over more and more work of the priests, teaching the faith, baptising and even at times – quite without authority – celebrating the eucharist, Rome became seriously alarmed. In January 1980, the Pope invited the seven Dutch bishops, who by now were sharply divided, to discuss the situation with him. Although five of the bishops were broadly in favour of the developments and only two were opposed, the Pope supported the conservatives. Since then, Professor Schillebeckx has had to answer several queries about his work in Rome. And each time a diocese has become vacant in Holland, the Pope has appointed a bishop who can be relied upon to hold firm to traditional viewpoints.

Well, how has all this affected the progress towards Christian unity in Holland? Cardinal Simonis of Utrecht, for one, has been making moves to stop Protestants from taking communion at Catholic Masses. He also wants Catholics to stop taking communion at Protestant services. The short-term effect of these and other moves has been to check and disturb ecumenical gatherings. Rome's argument, when unpacked, is that it is intellectually and spiritually dishonest to take part in the key celebration of unity with non-Catholic Christians when fundamental doctrinal differences remain. This position is, in fact, shared by Dr Paisley. But neither Rome nor Dr Paisley accepts that for many Christians two facts leap over these arguments: the first is that people who break church rules and share in communion services are convinced of the presence of Christ in these gatherings; and the second, that the church was founded not by a book of canon law, but by the Holy Spirit. There is a growing nervousness in Holland that in Rome, Christian Unity is seen as all other Christians coming round to Rome's point of view.

4 May 1985

Papal Bull

Let me begin by telling a story. It's about apostolic succession – that doctrine held dear by some Christians, that bishops are the true successors of the first apostles. They are linked with Peter and James and the rest, it's believed, by an unbroken chain through the centuries created by bishop consecrating bishop. The story goes that one day an Anglican was being shown round Vatican City by a pope. In the gardens were some hens. 'These hens', the Pope is supposed to have said, 'are direct descendants of the cock that crowed when Peter betrayed our Lord.' 'Ah,' said the Anglican, 'but are they good layers?'

This story is sometimes told in clerical circles to back up the notion that Anglicans are more interested in apostolic success than apostolic succession.

Well, a fair number of Christians would regard the Church of England as not exactly a record layer at the moment. Moreover some Anglicans are still very concerned about matters like apostolic succession and being properly recognised as a church by Rome. But the fact is that at present, technically speaking, Roman Catholics still do not recognise the Archbishop of Canterbury or any Anglican clergy as really priests.

This week an exchange of letters was published in Rome and London which suggested a way forward on this, one of the most difficult issues in Anglican-Roman Catholic relations.

At the heart of the problem is a judgement made in 1896 by Pope Leo XIII, declaring that Anglican ordinations were 'absolutely null and utterly void'. This was declared in a bull, as such papal edicts are so splendidly called, named *Apostolicae Curae*.

The Pope believed that the form of service used to ordain Anglican clergy was inadequate. This was because it omitted words making it plain that priests had the power to consecrate and offer the 'true body and blood of Christ', in a sacrifice which was more than just a way of remembering the crucifixion.

It appears that the Pope was unaware that on those grounds many clergy in the early centuries of the church were also invalidly ordained. For instance, the Roman ritual for ordaining priests in the third century contains no reference whatever to the power of offering sacrifice. Anyway, the papal bull was declared, and ever since has caused problems.

You might ask, why does all this matter? Well, the fact is that a number of Anglican priests mind deeply that they are not recognised as priests by Rome. But secondly, and much more important, is the goal that Anglicans and Roman Catholics should one day be able to take full part in each other's communion services. It's especially painful for couples in mixed Roman Catholic-Anglican marriages to be unable to share communion. Official Roman recognition of Anglican priests would obviously be a major step forward towards solving this.

A letter published this week from the head of the Vatican Secretariat for Promoting Christian Unity, Cardinal Johannes Willebrands, suggests that the way forward is for the two churches to agree to a shared statement of what they believe about ministry and about the communion service. This, the cardinal says, would be 'the strongest possible stimulus' to finding a solution to the present obstacles blocking Rome's recognition of Anglican orders. Such a statement of belief has already been drawn up by the Anglo-Roman Catholic International Commission (ARCIC). This is now being assessed by the two churches.

The cardinal sent his letter to the two co-chairmen of the present international commission. In their reply they added the point that the ordination of women priests in some Anglican churches abroad has created 'a fresh and grave obstacle' to reconciliation, but they remain hopeful and confident of success.

Movement is possible for a number of reasons. The most important is that there's a new mood, and less of the fortress mentality, in Rome. But any development on either side is accompanied by protests from those who suspect a sell-out. The Church Society, an Anglican evangelical group, is talking about splitting off from the Church of England if it endorses the prepared Anglican-Roman Catholic statements on ministry and the eucharist. On the other wing, some conservative Roman Catholics are also unhappy about the way things seem to be moving. Progress is a slow business. But if the church insists on digging holes for itself to fall into, it's likely to take a lot of laborious effort to climb out.

8 March 1986

Bishop's Move

If you walk around the quiet elegant back streets of Westminster, you may come across a fine house which is almost completely boarded up. This is the home and offices of the Bishop of London, the Right Reverend Graham Leonard, who is at present on a curious visit to America, extending the bounds of his jurisdiction. He has conducted a confirmation service in Tulsa, Oklahoma, at a parish which is in dispute with its local Anglican bishop.

Before his departure I suggested to him, tongue in cheek, that the boarded scaffolding might be there to protect him from fellow bishops and others who disapprove of what they see as his interference in other people's business. He laughed and said no, the house was being painted. But in some ways the boarding is an interesting symbol of how his headquarters are becoming a fortress in an ecclesiastical war between traditionalists and liberals in the church.

Dr Leonard himself insists that he and the Archbishop of Canterbury are still friends despite their disagreements over the Tulsa case. And when you meet him in his small book-lined study, puffing away at his pipe like an unpretentious and friendly headmaster rather enjoying the publicity, it's hard to see him as the rebel and hard man that he's sometimes portrayed as being. Some Anglicans are wondering rhetorically whether he has gone mad in deciding so firmly to reject the advice of the archbishop and forty-seven of his brother bishops here, not to mention the whole house of American bishops, who tell him not to interfere. But others are delighted that he's taken what they see as a stand of principle in supporting the American priest of the parish concerned. Although he's been deposed by the Church of England's sister church in America, the Episcopal Church, for putting church money into a separate religious foundation, the priest's supporters say the real reason for his deposition is his opposition to changes in the American church in worship, in doctrine and over the ordination of women priests.

So what kind of man is the Bishop of London? He's the son of a clergyman of low church views and was educated at an evangelical public school, going up to Balliol to read science. During the war he was an army captain. Later he was ordained, and he moved away from the low church wing of the Church of England, to become an Anglo-Catholic – the branch of the Church of England that is closest to Rome, with a high view of the sacraments and of church tradition, as well as the authority of the Bible. He and his wife Priscilla, sister of Sir Michael Swann, former chairman of the BBC board of governors, have two sons.

In the 1960s he successfully opposed a scheme for Anglican-Methodist unity. He became Bishop of Willesden, then Bishop of Truro, reaching London in 1981. Since then he has become a leader of those opposed to the ordination of women priests.

Just over a year ago, after a conference of a hundred priests at New College, Oxford, he said he would be available to do what was right in the event of a church split over women priests. This was interpreted to mean that if it came to it, he would be prepared to lead an alternative church, and it inspired near-devotion among some Anglo-Catholics, who felt that until then their backs were to the wall. In the rooms of the organiser of that conference afterwards, he was given a glass of brandy. As he handed back his empty glass on leaving, one of the priests wondered jubilantly whether the glass should be kept, un-washed, as a memento of an historic occasion.

Yet in other circles he is described as dull, uncharismatic, dogmatic and unimaginative. Certainly he is a man who is firm in his beliefs and proud of his principles. But the odd thing is that pastorally, except on the women priests issue, he's regarded as generous, even soft. He strongly opposes homosexuality, yet one clergyman of his diocese has accused him publicly of making his diocese in fact a safe haven for aggressively homosexual priests.

Even on political issues, it's hard to label him simply. He is certainly conservative in outlook, and broadly supports the government's defence policy, for instance. Yet he is opposed to the government on the Nationality Bill, on the destruction of the GLC and on the abolition of Sunday trading laws.

But perhaps the key to understanding him is this. He believes the Anglican church is only part of the universal church, and therefore does not have the authority to make changes, like the introduction of women priests, without the agreement of the Roman Catholics and the Eastern Orthodox. It's ironic therefore that the vast majority of his brother bishops think that by adopting the Tulsa parish, he is encouraging schism.

1 November 1986

Dead Wood?

Tomorrow sees the start of the annual, worldwide week of prayer for Christian unity. And as part of the preparations for this, interchurch councils have been meeting from Little Middlecombe in the Muddle to as far afield as Nairobi and Alice Springs, planning shared services of prayer for a better future together.

One account of such a meeting was included in this week's issue of the Catholic newspaper, *The Universe*, in its column titled 'The Secret Diary of Father Hadrian Mule, aged 55 and three-quarters'.

'Arrived late at Council of Churches meeting', Father Mule

reports. 'Usually as controversial as Knitting Guild Tea Party, but today sparks fly as some want to serve sherry at a reception to the horror of others who regard alcohol as fruit juice gone bad. Some non-Catholics are hurt at their inability to receive communion at the planned Mass for unity and express their hurt forcibly. Others with equal force say they will never share in the Mass anyway. 'I', writes Father Mule, 'am irritable and impatient, and show it. But after the meeting there's real warmth and friendship.'

Certainly church unity can still seem a million miles away, despite the intensified, well-meaning efforts over the next few days. In Northern Ireland, 'church unity' is one of those phrases that still echo emptily. 'Dialogue', as I once heard Ian Paisley roar, 'smacks too much of dead wood.' But there really is progress towards it in other parts of the UK. Relations between church leaders are often cordial. In Liverpool, for instance, as everyone knows, Dr David Shepherd, the Anglican bishop, and Monsignor Derek Worlock, the Roman Catholic archbishop, have joined with their Free Church colleagues to do as much of their work as they possibly can together. And there are well over 400 so-called local ecumenical projects in England. But there are still difficulties. The British Council of Churches has not yet been given any great authority by its twenty-eight member churches. The Catholics indeed, though they send observers, are still not members at all. And the recent general synod meeting of the Anglicans, which discussed the progress of the international Anglican-Roman Catholic theological talks, showed how tetchy lots of Anglicans still are over Catholic doctrines such as infallibility and the immaculate conception of the Virgin Mary.

So has the momentum towards church unity run down? Well, I think it is just moving into a much more realistic stage. Last Lent, in association with over fifty local and national radio stations, the churches launched an ecumenical course that involved nearly a million believers. From this the message seems to be that people long for church unity, but anything that smacks of uniformity is out. They are proud of their own traditions, but they want to get to know other people's traditions better and to share in and benefit from them. So I think a number of joint services this week should be well attended.

The Lent course showed that in many places, it was felt that the *clergy* were the ones who held back in moves towards unity. I expect Father Hadrian Mule, aged fifty-five and three-quarters, will now be remembering all those interchurch council meetings he's attended over the years, and sighing deeply at man's ingratitude.

17 January 1987

4

MANY FAITHS,
MANY PATHS

Lord Krishna

This holiday weekend if the weather does its duty, hundreds of thousands of us will be making our way to the beaches for a swim. Next week in India thousands of Hindu pilgrims will be bathing in the river Ganges or some other local sacred river or piece of water. That's not just a way of cooling down, but a religious act of purification. It's related to a festival known as Rakshabandhan, in which sisters and brothers exchange signs of affection. Rakshabandhan means ties of security. These ties, known popularly as raki, are coloured cotton or silk threads with a little decoration. A sister ties them to her brother's wrist, as a reminder to him to look after her. In return the brother gives her a present of cash or perhaps a piece of clothing or jewellery.

But around the world Hindus are also celebrating the birthday of the Lord Krishna 3,400 years ago. One scholar said that trying to describe Hinduism was like being a blind man trying to describe an elephant. For Hinduism is a religion which, although followed by hundreds of millions around the world, has no defining creed, no group of exclusive followers, and no centralised hierarchy. Essentially, however, Hinduism involves the worship of the gods Vishnu or Siva, or the goddess Shakti, and their various forms, aspects, spouses and children. Krishna is one aspect of the god Vishnu.

During this festival, families remind each other of the story of Krishna's birth and life. Krishna was born at a time when India was in chaos. It was divided into numerous kingdoms and many of its rulers wielded their power unjustly and cruelly. Among the most vicious was King Kamsa. He had a cousin destined to be Krishna's parent. On the wedding day of Krishna's parents, Kamsa had a premonition that he would be killed by their child. He imprisoned them and murdered each of their children as it was born. The night the eighth child, Krishna, was born, a storm was blowing outside. But tradition has it he was delivered in calm and peace. By a miracle the prison guards were asleep, so following the command of a voice from heaven, Krishna's father took the child to a neighbouring village and exchanged it for the baby daughter of a friend.

When King Kamsa heard the news of the birth of the child, he rushed round to the prison to kill the baby. Furious at the sight of the child, he was about to throw her against a rock, when the child slipped from his hand and he heard a heavenly voice saying that the one who would kill him was growing elsewhere. According to one version, he ordered a slaughter of the innocents at the child's birth, an action reported in the Bible to have been imitated much later by King Herod at the birth of another saviour. Anyway, sure enough later in Krishna's life, he killed the king.

The stories about Krishna are full of humanity and humour and divinity. Some years ago, on one of those grey dank winter evenings that make you feel like emigrating, I saw an Indian woman dance some of the tales. The building was a dilapidated old music-hall in London's East End, with paint peeling off the walls. She was dressed in the traditional costume of vivid reds and golds, and wearing bells on her ankles. She told through dance how Krishna as a mischievous child steals the clothes of the village girls as they're bathing in the river. Like all Hindu stories, it's not as simple as it first appears. On one level, it's just a folk tale about a child's game. On another it's about the relationship of the god Krishna with his people. The dancer said it was a parable about loving and being loved by God and how he sometimes hides from his people and sometimes forces them into a direct encounter with him.

As an adolescent, Krishna was an amorous cowherd playing a flute. Later, grown to manhood, he married, had children and grandchildren and is supposed to have lived to the age of 120. Whether as wrestler, wise adviser, statesman, or strategist, he is reputed to have solved many problems – from local water supplies to great battles. His task was always to support the righteous and put down the wicked. True religion, he said, meant seeing God in ourselves, in each other and in all things.

No wonder Hindus speak his name with love and respect. Krishna eventually died when a hunter, mistaking him for a deer in the forest, shot him in the heel – his one vulnerable spot. Achilles, you may remember, had a similar problem.

To all Hindus, best wishes for your birthday celebrations.

25 August 1984

If Only My People . . .

Happy New Year. Some of you may find that a shade premature, to say the least. But this week Jewish and Islamic communities around the world have been celebrating their respective New Years. Muslims have been exchanging stories about the prophet Muhammad. In Jewish synagogues in Britain, Israel and elsewhere, congregations have been hearing the blowing of the ram's horn which calls to mind Abraham's sacrifice of a ram in place of his son, and they've been joining in the haunting music of the prayers.

Rosh Hashanah, the Jewish New Year, is a time of reflection and penitence. Its keynotes are faith and hope. Suitably enough hope and faith are very much the keynotes of a new book out this month by the distinguished Chief Rabbi of the British Commonwealth, Sir Immanuel Jakobovits. It's called *If Only My People* . . . and it's an account of Zionism in his life. The title was meant to show clearly that he was speaking as a rabbi, not as a politician. It refers to the psalm where the Lord says, 'If only my people would listen to me, and Israel would walk in my ways, I would soon subdue their enemies.' The book is in a sense an appeal for Jews everywhere, and particularly in Israel, to return to the moral ideals which are at the heart of Judaism. For how else, asks the Chief Rabbi, has this small scattered nation survived over 3,000 years of chequered and sometimes agonised history?

Jewish religious ideas are so embedded in contemporary civilisation that it's hard to imagine a time when they were absent. When you think about it, the Jewish nation was the first to declare belief in a single unified God, the first to proclaim values like defending the weak and befriending the stranger. It is in Judaism that the roots of Christianity and Islam – those new young things – lie. The ideas that first emerged in Jewish religious life, transformed the ancient world, and eventually ended it for ever. It was Judaism that introduced the Twilight of the Gods.

Over the centuries the moral vision of Judaism – however endangered in times of persecution – has been maintained by individual Jews: doctors who've worked for the benefit of mankind, musicians, artists, thinkers, scientists, people who've felt called because of their Jewishness to fulfil a particular destiny.

Central to the Chief Rabbi's book is a warning against what he sees as two dangerous tendencies in Judaism today. The first is the sort of secular Zionism which regards Israel merely as a dumping ground for homeless Jewish refugees. The second is the politicisation of religion.

Earlier this year I was in Israel for Passover, when Jews celebrate God's deliverance of their people from slavery in Egypt. I met someone there who demonstrated the tensions of being both Jewish and atheist. He and his family and other non-religious friends wanted to celebrate the Passover meal as a symbol of their Jewishness. Yet they could not accept the key figure, God. Their compromise was to turn Passover into a secular celebration of liberation.

But to Sir Immanuel, Israel must represent more than this.

To him it's the place where Jews must work together to try to fulfil the religious vision of a nation being the people of God. That means creating a society where those who suffer are treated generously and compassionately, where families stay together, where vandalism and murder fade away, where the stranger is treated honourably. To him, it would be a failure if Israel were to become just like any other state. And in the book, he shows himself to be worried by and critical of what he sees as narrow Israeli secular nationalism, just as he is compassionate towards the sufferings of the Palestinian refugees.

He places a good bit of the responsibility for what he would see as a moral vacuum in some of Israeli life at the doorstep of his own colleagues, the rabbis, regarding some of those who have become immersed in party politics as prostituting religious values. Certainly the way minority religious parties in Israel have held successive governments over a barrel and forced them to make financial and legal concessions, coercing the secular majority to go along with their views, seems a sorry and at times shameful story. For Sir Immanuel, the notion of coercing people rather than persuading people is hopelessly counterproductive. As I read this section in his book, I was reminded of a similar statement in Bishop David Jenkins's controversial sermon at his enthronement service in Durham Cathedral last weekend: 'God does not impose himself,' he reminded the congregation, 'he gives himself.'

For anyone who wants to be challenged by and illuminated about the Jewish moral vision, this book will be a guiding light.

29 September 1984

ECHO

In between the blare of the traffic down London's Oxford Street, and some other high streets in Britain, you can sometimes hear in the distance sounds of drums, cymbals and chanting. A few minutes later, a group of people with cropped heads, and wearing sandals and loose eastern-style orange robes, may come slowly into sight, clapping, dancing and chanting. These are members of the Hare Krishna movement – a movement which now has temples in more than twenty western countries. These temples are run by westerners who've been won over to the Hindu religion. They are a branch of an incredibly diverse religion which, world-wide, has more than 500 million followers.

Last Tuesday, in an elegant room in the Waldorf Hotel in London, a representative of the Hare Krishna movement, dressed in white, His Grace Hari Krishna Das, who was born in Holland of Dutch parents, joined with four representatives of the wider Hindu community in Britain. They were all there to launch publicly in the UK a new body called the European Council of Hindu Organisations, or ECHO. The council was founded in Paris in February at a meeting of fifteen representatives of Hindu organisations in western Europe. It hopes to be able to put pressure on centres of European power on behalf of Hindus living in Europe.

The meeting was an interesting sign of how the Hare Krishna movement – regarded by many people in Britain as just another of those new religious movements lumped together and labelled as sects or cults – has come to be increasingly accepted by the Hindu community as part of itself.

The new council claims that there are now over 3 million people in Europe who practise the Hindu way of life – it wants the governments to recognise this and make certain changes accordingly. For instance, in law courts, they say, Hindus should be able to take the oath on a copy of their own sacred scriptures, not the Bible. They would like to be able, throughout Europe, to set up their own schools, and to influence the content of teaching in state schools and colleges. They want the main Hindu festivals to be included automatically in calendars and diaries along with Christian and other festivals. They would also like more time on radio and television devoted to Hindu affairs and beliefs as of right.

Several speakers emphasised that their vision is of a society guided not by material needs, but by spiritual values.

But the news conference on Tuesday illustrated some of the problems. About fifty or so people were there – among them a very senior diplomat from the Indian High Commission. But only two members of the national non-Hindu press attended. When this was discovered, the editor of the Hindu paper *New Life*, C. B. Patel, sprang to his feet and with tongue firmly in cheek, amused the gathered company by urging them to arrange a demonstration and a scuffle or two outside the Indian High Commission. The national press, he implied, was only interested in Hindu affairs if violence was part of the outcome.

The chairman of the new council, Mr Vidya Anand, said he believed there were now more than a million people following a Hindu way of life in the United Kingdom. The concerns of these people should, he said, be reflected – after all they pay their taxes, licence fees and the rest. His words reminded me strongly of the sort of views expressed within similar organisations set up by Muslims in Britain.

Some people claim that a closer estimate of the number of Hindus in the UK is half a million rather than a million. But it's still a sizeable number. But one problem is the fragmentation of the Hindu and Muslim communities. Immigrants have come from different countries with different languages and sometimes different theologies. There are sometimes different factions. That's why some leaders within the Muslim and Hindu communities have tried to set up groups like this new council, so that they can move towards a more unified voice. But it's often a slow business. And opinion is often divided. The Muslim community in Britain, for instance, has a range of views on the schools question. Some believe that Islamic schools are vital for the protection of the faith. Others believe it more important that Muslim children go to school with children of other faiths. In 1984 a small fee-paying primary school run by the Hare Krishna movement was given approval by inspectors of the Department of Education. But some applications for schools have been turned down. It's not always clear to the religious community concerned why this is so.

Organisations like the new council can clearly have a role in the future, but they do need strong support from the religious people concerned, and a clear, realistic programme of action. *9 March 1985*

Adam, Abraham and Islam

If by any chance you get stuck in a holiday traffic jam this weekend, you might be a bit consoled to remember that somewhere in Saudi Arabia there is certainly one very much worse. For over the last few days, well over a million people from all over the world have poured into the city of Mecca and its surrounding desert. And there traffic jams really are tough. For you can be melting in a sizzling car with a temperature outside as high as 120° Fahrenheit. The visitors are all in Mecca on pilgrimage. And these holidays really are holy-days. The visitors have come to fulfil the commandment of Muhammad the Prophet, following the Koran, that at least once in a lifetime every Muslim who is well enough and rich enough should make a pilgrimage to Mecca. It's not that God is to be found *only* in Mecca and the various holy sites around. For Muslims, God is in everything, in each object, in every person. It's just that the pilgrimage to Mecca concentrates the mind wonderfully.

The name of the pilgrimage – Hajj – means 'effort'. And no wonder. The pilgrimage certainly demands both physical and spiritual effort. But talk to almost any Muslim who's returned from the Hajj, and they will tell you that despite the pressures of the crowds and the heat, they came away with a new sense of unity and divine mercy which has refreshed their daily lives. In the old days, people would arrive, as the Koran says, on 'swift camels'. These days it's more likely to be a jet plane. On arrival in Saudi Arabia the men don two simple white pieces of cloth as a symbol of renouncing worldly things, and as a sign that in the eyes of God, prince and beggar are as one. Women, too, dress simply. They then travel into Mecca, where no non-Muslims may enter and where all forms of violence, even picking a flower, are forbidden. There they will see the great temple with the minarets piercing the sky, towards which all Muslims turn when they say their prayers. In the central courtyard is the Kaaba, an empty cubic building on the site where Abraham is believed to have built the first temple to God. After this they run seven times between two hillocks in a re-enactment of the search for water in the desert by Hagar the wife of Abraham.

A few miles outside Mecca is a vast plain, called the plain of Arafat (not to be confused with Mount Ararat in Turkey). There Abraham is said to have decided to defy Satan and submit to God by preparing to sacrifice his son Ishmael, who later became the father of nations. Tomorrow this dusty plain surrounded by hills will be a mass of tents and people dressed in white. They will stand praying to God for mercy and forgiveness and purity. There will be Muslims from all over the Islamic world – Pakistan, Iran, Iraq, America, Europe, even China. Some will have walked and worked their way from as far as western Africa. Old and young, people of so many races and languages will *en route* have shared their food, told each other about their lives, exchanged jokes and helped each other along. It's on the plain in prayer that most pilgrims seem to experience the most overwhelming sense of unity under God. Cultural, class and national barriers for a few hours are dissolved in a taste of the harmony Muslims believe that God wants for the world.

In recent years some Iranian demonstrators have tried to make the celebration political as well as religious, but the Saudi police have dealt firmly with disturbances and most pilgrims want the Hajj to continue as it has done in the past.*

For Muslims all this area not only has associations with Abraham, and with the Prophet Muhammad who was born in Mecca fourteen hundred years ago, but also with Adam, the first man. Muslim legend has it that it was here that Adam first fell to earth from heaven. God urged Adam to seek the divine throne on earth. In the desert he discovered the navel of the earth, the place round which the earth had spun as it came into being. There he saw a throne with four emerald pillars and roofed with a giant ruby. Underneath the canopy was a pearly white stone like a resplendent star, 'light upon light' according to the Koran. This was the symbol of Adam's soul.

Today the Kaaba is for Muslims the symbol of the place where the heavenly bliss touches the earth most directly. It is, too, a symbol of the soul. For what could be a better throne for God on earth than the hearts of men and women?

24 August 1985

Can We Trust the Gospels?

First, just a word to those who wrote to me following my talk about Adam and Abraham and Islam. They wondered whether Muslims really believe that it was his son Ishmael that the patriarch Abraham was prepared to sacrifice. As they rightly pointed out, Genesis, chapter 22, speaks of the son called Isaac. The answer is that the Koran and the Bible diverge. If you're a Christian you follow one account, and if you're a Muslim, you follow the other.

Divergences in the sacred writings of both religions – of which this is one of several examples – have over the centuries caused a great deal of trouble. And Christians who have been involved in serious conversations about faith with Muslims

---

* Two years later, all went wrong – 400 people died in clashes between Iranian pilgrims and Saudi security forces.

sometimes find that when Christians quote from the gospels, Muslims reply that the text they are quoting from is not the true gospel. The original gospel of Jesus Christ, they claim, has been lost, and past generations of Christians have so corrupted the Christian scriptures that they are now useless. It is this sort of argument that recently was being enthusiastically declared around Britain by a touring Muslim evangelist. He believed that Jesus presented himself as an ordinary prophet, that he never died on the cross, but was spirited away by angels – and that he announced the coming of Muhammad.

One recent book pinpoints the start of this process of the so-called falsification of biblical texts as the Council of Nicaea in AD 325. It claims that this was the first really well-organised attempt to suppress Jesus' original teaching. And this was done by choosing as the official gospels of the church only four out of 300 or so available at the time.

Not surprisingly, these attacks on the authenticity of the Bible texts as we have them are distressing to Christians, and a major obstacle to improving relations between the two faiths. For they pose the question: 'Can we trust the gospels?'

Well, that's the title of a thoughtful and fascinating leaflet which has been written to try to get over this apparent obstacle. It's published by the Catholic Truth Society and its author is a Roman Catholic priest and scholar, Father Hans Wijngaards. Father Wijngaards says that if Muslims keep on repeating the old accusations, they may well believe they are right. A frog in a well may believe he has seen the ocean. Genuine progress in dialogue, he continues, is when both Christians and Muslims are prepared to step outside the vicious circle of self-enforced prejudice and face objective facts. And he says objective fact is that for four centuries after Muhammad, no Muslim theologian seriously contended that the gospel texts were not authentic. In the Koran, Muslims are told to respect the gospel revealed to Jesus Christ. The questioning of the texts began in Spain in the eleventh century. A vizier ruling the south of Spain came up against some of the contradictions – for instance, the verse which says, 'They slew him not and they crucified him not.'

Since the Koran must be true, he argued, the gospel texts must be wrong. Therefore they must have been doctored by Christians. And over the years, various legends developed – a number of them portraying Paul as a crafty hypocrite and corrupter.

Well, is there any way we can now know what the original gospel texts written down between AD 50 and AD 90 really said? Over the last hundred years or so, numerous scientists have worked at answering this question. They have masses of material available – there are no fewer than 4,680 manuscripts of the Greek text. Then there are over 6,000 manuscripts of ancient translations in other languages, ranging from the second to the fourteenth century. The repeated copying of them has of course introduced some variations. But by comparing the manuscripts and tracing them back, the scientists now believe that 98.5 per cent of the original text is certain beyond reasonable doubt.

Christians interested in dialogue with Muslims are now asking Muslims to accept these results of modern scientific scholarship. They believe that in a world where materialism seems to get stronger, now is the time for Christians and Muslims to explore together what they have in common – their belief in one God, the creator and source of all revelation. The Pope certainly seemed to have this in mind, when recently he met Muslims in Africa. But for real conversation each party needs to respect the value the other places on the sacred writings of his or her religion. Rubbishing the other person's sacred texts, whether the Bible or the Koran, gets nowhere.

31 August 1985

Rabbit but No Pork

Towards the end of last year a group of 120 Christians from various backgrounds – Catholic, Free Church, Greek Orthodox and Anglican – spent three days and nights sharing Jewish life and worship. The purpose was to help them to understand better what living Judaism is all about. The highly successful visits to Jewish homes were organised by the Leo Baeck College in North London, which is the cultural centre of the Jewish progressive movement in Britain, and the visits are just another sign of growing friendship and mutual interest between some Jewish and Christian circles.

Jewish-Christian dialogue – as opposed to confrontation – is a relatively new thing, although you can trace instances of toleration and generosity from the first century onwards.

A centre for the study of Judaism and Jewish-Christian relations has now been established in the Selly Oak colleges in Birmingham. Its director is Rabbi Dr Norman Solomon, and last year, in a lecture, he reviewed the current state of play. He pointed out that although the book of Acts in the New Testament quotes a rabbi speaking tolerantly of the followers of Jesus, toleration in matters of faith proceeded slowly, as often backwards as forwards.

When John Locke wrote his famous epistle on toleration at the end of the seventeenth century, he took the precaution of publishing it under a pseudonym. And even Locke was not prepared to tolerate atheists or Roman Catholics.

It's really only in the last forty years that Christian-Jewish dialogue has borne fruit in the form of direct open consultations and formal guidelines issued by leading church bodies. So why the change of mood?

Well, the answers are complex. One of the reasons Dr Solomon has identified is that improved communications and transport have made people more aware of different cultures and religions. Secondly, there has this century been a gradual but remarkable revolution in modern critical study of the Bible. As people have gradually come to realise the need to understand the Bible in its historical context, there has been a spate of academic books about Jesus as a Jew, and on first-century Judaism. Whereas most Christians have a notion of Pharisaism as a cold heartless doctrine, nit-picking over points of law, some recent scholarly books have portrayed a religion of the Pharisees which was in fact built on the love of God and of man. The implication of some of this new scholarship is that Jesus was not a rebel against the best of Jewish religion at all.

Two other factors have had an effect – the traumatic impact of the Second World War and the concentration camps, and the establishment of the state of Israel.

Many Christians are aware that despite the heroic minority of Christians who helped and sheltered Jews in the 1930s and 1940s, often with fearful danger to themselves and their own families, the majority of Christians were silent, compliant, even acquiescent at what was happening. One result since has been an intense soul-searching. But on this Rabbi Solomon is brutally realistic. He declares that no enduring and healthy relationship between people is built on guilt. If it leads to a new relationship all to the good, but it must be based on genuine understanding, mutual love and respect.

So what sort of dialogue is desired? In 1983, the Chief Rabbi, Sir Immanuel Jakobovits, made it clear that the Jewish community – certainly the Orthodox Jews – did not want theological dialogue in the narrow sense of one side scrutinising critically the other's beliefs. Nor did it want joint religious services.

Instead he focused on two other areas. One was the whole question of social and moral issues. This was an area which Jews and Christians could explore together, finding *common* approaches to issues which challenged religious leadership and the religious conscience. The second area where progress could be made, he suggested, was in developing a realistic relationship with each other. And central to that, was that Christians must begin to accept and understand the importance to Jews of the restoration to them of the land of Israel after nineteen centuries of national homelessness. I might add here that the Vatican's continued refusal to recognise the state of Israel on grounds that its borders are not yet fixed is still a source of hurt to many Jews.

One of the complications in all this is the danger that some Christians who get fascinated by Jesus the Jew, begin to imagine that modern-day Judaism is essentially the same as that practised by Jews in first-century Palestine. In fact Judaism has adapted and deepened through the influence of Jewish commentators and teachers over the centuries. Christians have much yet to learn.

4 January 1986

When in Rome . . .

This week I discovered the origin of the saying 'When in Rome do as the Romans do'. It dates back to the fourth century when the mother of St Augustine emigrated from North Africa to Milan. At that time it was common for North African Christians and citizens of Rome to fast on Saturdays. She was disturbed to discover that this was not the case in Milan. The local bishop, St Ambrose, suggested that she should not fast on Saturdays in Milan, but when in Rome do as the Romans do.

The issues raised by this well-known saying provide the framework to a fascinating book published earlier this year, which deals with the knotty question of the legal and human rights of ethnic minorities living in Britain. Called *English Law and Ethnic Minority Customs*, its author is Sebastian Poulter, senior lecturer in Law at the University of Southampton. He explains concisely a wide variety of customs, ranging from polygamy to female circumcision to worship. He then analyses how the law relates to them, and gives details of the most significant legal cases. Finally he assesses the scope for legal reform. For days now I've been dipping in and out of it enthralled by the scholarship it displays and the human and practical problems involved in applying the ideals of religious freedom.

Of course religious toleration is a fairly recent idea in Britain. Under the sixteenth-century Act of Supremacy, for instance, all judges, magistrates and mayors had to take an oath of allegiance to the crown which no Roman Catholic could conscientiously swear because it denied the spiritual power of the Pope.

These days, the vast majority of people in this country if asked in an opinion poll whether they favoured freedom of religion, would say unhesitatingly, 'Yes.' But does that include freedom to worship *alone* or together with others? And what happens if that religious freedom infringes the rights of other people? Such questions emerged sharply in the following case.

Mr Ahmad, a devout Muslim, was employed as a full-time teacher by the Inner London Education Authority in a series of schools. On Friday afternoons in 1974 he began regularly attending a nearby mosque for early afternoon prayers. This meant he returned to the school some three-quarters of an hour late. In consequence, because of timetable difficulties, he had no duties on Friday afternoons at all. This caused some resentment among other teachers. When the ILEA suggested he take a new contract and be paid for four and a half days' work a week, not five, he took the case to court. At the court of appeal, Lord Scarman backed him. He argued that the Education Act of 1944 now had to be interpreted in the context of the multiracial society which had accepted international obligations and enacted statutes to eliminate discrimination on grounds of race, religion, colour, or sex. He said that if the Act was interpreted narrowly, that would mean that a Muslim who took his religion seriously could never accept employment as a full-time teacher. This he regarded as quite unacceptable. In Lord Scarman's view the education authorities should be flexible.

But Judge Orr thought Lord Scarman's conclusion would authorise what was technically a breach of contract. And Lord Denning's view was that if the rights of others, in this case other teachers, were jeopardised, then freedom of worship had to be restricted.

Finally the case went to the European Commission on Human Rights. The commission dealt with three key issues. First of all it had little difficulty in recognising that freedom of worship meant being free to worship with *others* and not just alone. But it then went on to ask how vital was the Islamic injunction to worship in a mosque on Fridays. For eight years when Mr Ahmad had worked much further away from the mosque, he had not visited it, because it was unrealistic to do so given the terms of his employment. So in that case why did he have to break his contract now – even by three-quarters of an hour a week? Finally the commission dealt with the question of what limitations could in fact be placed on the right to freedom of worship. The commission felt this right was not absolute, that the education authority was entitled to rely on the contract being met, and that it had tried to accommodate Mr Ahmad's needs by offering him the $4^{1}/_{2}$-day week. And so Mr Ahmad lost his case.

Compared with some other cases in Sebastian Poulter's book, that is a fairly straightforward one. But it brought home to me the complexity of the arguments about human rights in a multi-faith society.

6 December 1986

5

SYNOD

SENTENCES

Weary Women

Next week, 550 members of the Church of England will be sloshing their way through the fallen leaves in Dean's Yard Westminster, making their way to Church House for the autumn session of the General Synod. One of the issues to be discussed this time is whether in the next few years, some of the faces on the benches of the House of Clergy could be the faces of women. On Thursday, the Bishop of Southwark, Dr Ronald Bowlby, will, at the request of the local synod of his diocese, urge the General Synod to introduce legislation that would lead to the ordination of women as priests.

Of course, this is not a new subject. In 1975 a majority of the synod declared that there were no fundamental objections to the ordination of women, but the time was not ripe. The question being asked next week is: 'Is the time ripe now?'

Things have moved on since then – for better or for worse, depending on your views about women priests. Since 1975, the Anglican churches in America, New Zealand, Kenya, Uganda, Brazil and Canada have been ordaining women. There are now more than 600 women priests in the Anglican communion worldwide. Secondly, the majority of Church of England members are in favour of women priests. The latest poll just out shows that 66 per cent of people interviewed who go to church once a week and 80 per cent of people who worship in church about once a month, were in favour. Thirdly, whereas most of the *bishops* have long backed the ordination of women, there are now signs that more and more male *priests* are actively campaigning for it. Before the last synod, more than 700 of them signed an open letter to the archbishops of Canterbury and York, indicating their support.

So the mood has changed. And that's why members of the Movement for the Ordination of Women, known as MOW, want to restart the debate now. They know that next year this particular synod comes to the end of its five-year life, and new elections for members will have to be held before the final vote on any legislation. In these elections MOW supporters have to bring about a small but vital change in the membership of the House of Clergy. Without this small swing, it is thought the legislation will fail to get the required two-thirds majority in all three houses – bishops, lay people and clergy.

Needless to say, the opponents of the ordination of women are perfectly well aware how vital these elections will be. And their campaigning has begun too. It entered a new phase recently with the publication of a book by the Reverend William Oddie. This book, called *What Will Happen To God?*, explores the implications of some of the new Christian feminist theology which has been developing here and in the United States. To him the implications are revolutionary, and not only damaging to the church, but dangerous. He claims that feminists want to demolish the Christian doctrine of the fatherhood of God. On the front cover of his book is the telling symbol of Edwina Sandys's controversial sculpture of a crucified woman on the cross . . . the sculptor named her work 'Christa'.

To Dr Oddie and his colleagues, a woman *cannot* be a priest because we understand God through male symbols and the priest represents God at the communion table. The supporters of women priests find the literalness of this argument astonishing. They say that God's being encompasses both sexes.

Dr Oddie's book, it seems to me, may have both good and bad effects. It's the first critical book I know of, published here, that even begins to take seriously the new and challenging feminist theology that has exploded in America. Feminists argue that he has fallen into trap after trap in his arguments in the book. But it seems to me he has made some interesting points about the positively anti-Christian trends of some radical feminist theology. The dangerous effect of his book is if it makes people imagine that the far shores of feminist theology are synonymous with the thinking of organisations like the Movement for the Ordination of Women. On the whole, MOW is so conservative a group, it is practically genteel. Most of its members are ordinary middle-of-the-road Anglicans who feel the church is wasting marvellous resources in continuing to refuse to ordain women. Most of them have come to that view not through theory, but through knowing some of the women who feel called by God to the priesthood. These are not women who go off dancing in the moonlight in feminist covens, but women some of whom have already spent a lifetime quietly and faithfully serving the church they know and love.

10 November 1984

Cold Comfort

Watching the Anglican General Synod meeting in Westminster this week was even more confusing than usual. I rather suspect that the reason a lot of the 550 members never speak at all, is either because they haven't managed to wade through the preparatory papers, named, for instance, GS Misc 202, or else because they're frightened of the standing orders. It was worse this week because you couldn't always even recognise your neighbours. Some were muffled up in overcoats and dark glasses. Not a new type of clerical dress, it turned out, or even a secret society, though the synod did decide to ask for a report about Freemasonry. The coats were merely a buffer against the cold and the dark glasses a protection against the glare of TV lights. Actually I can report that nearly all members are rather pro TV these days. This is because the lights heat up the temperature a degree or two.

On the whole the temperature of the debates remained fairly low. Most people didn't get hot under the collar even over the major debate on belief and the issues raised by the controversy over Bishop Jenkins of Durham. Most really did want to hear what others had to say. It did occur to me at one stage that Jesus might have wondered why they seemed to be intent on talking about his body, rather than getting on with living his risen life. I would have liked to have heard the Bishop of Durham on that, but he asked the Archbishop of Canterbury for advice whether or not to speak, and the archbishop advised against.

Listening to the Bishop of Durham *is* a bit like playing table tennis with someone who insists on serving six balls at once. But I was rather hoping he might be coaxed into giving a speech with one ball in play, all about God living and acting in our world through our relationships with each other. They call it in synod 'incarnational theology'.

At the mention of the subject of remarriage, exhaustion set in. The Archbishop of York proclaimed he was never going to make a speech on the subject again. And with a bit of luck he won't have to. After the years of wrangling, the synod has now left things as they were. Individual priests have the burden of decision whether or not to remarry a divorced person during the lifetime of a previous partner. Clergy can either choose to exercise their legal right to perform a remarriage, or refuse to do so because church regulations still technically remain in force prohibiting such marriages.

On the Warnock report's recommendation that experiments should be permitted on human embryos for the first fourteen days of life, slightly more people were opposed than were in favour. The debate reflected a lot of unease and uncertainty about the moral issues involved – a mood mirrored in the parliamentary debate too.

The debate on a private member's motion urging the government to reconsider the deployment of Cruise missiles turned out very strangely. Someone else tried to hijack the motion and turn it into a call for a nuclear freeze and for the government to reconsider the Trident programme. But in the end, by the tiniest of majorities, synod decided to put none of it to the vote. The most interesting speech, I thought, came from the Bishop of Salisbury, Dr John Austin Baker, who supported the move to call a halt to the debate before a vote. You might think this is rather strange from the man who chaired the committee that two years ago produced the report *The Church and the Bomb*, which recommended that Britain should abandon its independent nuclear deterrent. But he's now apparently come to the conclusion that motions like that are practically pointless.

So the bishop recommended a new approach for the church. This was to face the fact that Jesus laid on his followers the vocation of non-violence. So the church should give spiritual support to those who try to follow it. And next, the church should keep on pressing for answers to questions about policies that already exist. For instance, the British government says that its independent Polaris deterrent on its own is sufficiently powerful to deter the Soviet Union from attacking us. But if that is so, why then do we need parity between east and west at present levels of nuclear arms? It will be interesting to see whether his scepticism about resolutions will filter into other church assemblies.

16 February 1985

Purple Passage

I was thinking the other day that if I were led blindfold into a Christian assembly, I would soon know where I was because of the style of jokes. This week I've been watching the General Synod of the Church of England in action, and there is very definitely a particular brand of Anglican humour which is different from that of other denominations. To charm an Anglican assembly what you do is to go off to the library for an hour or two, get down the largest book you can find on church history and dig out some anecdote or other which will hinge on tensions between church and state.

The best sort always feature a bishop, preferably an arch-bishop, and a Prime Minister or a Queen. Let me quote you one such story that was told to synod this week by Dr Gary Bennett of Oxford University during a debate on the role of suffragan – that's junior – bishops. In 1839 Archbishop Howley received a unique distinction. He was the first archbishop to have the House of Lords vote that his speeches were incomprehensible. His mind was so full of practical details that he lost sight of the general principles. Sydney Smith, the great preacher and champion of parliamentary reform, said he reminded him of wheels in search of a carriage. When he was ushered into Queen Victoria's presence, to announce the news of her accession to the throne, the Duke of Wellington had to remind him why he had come. Now, Dr Bennett doesn't tell such stories without a point. And the point was that the debate he was listening to also reminded him of wheels without a carriage. It was so bogged down with discussion of administration and whether junior bishops need more secretarial help and better offices and so on, that the key question was being forgotten.

That was 'What should the role of bishops be?' Dr Bennett reminded synod that in the early church, the bishop was the chief pastor of a local Christian community. He was not an administrator, but a teacher, preacher, pastor and chief cele-brant of the sacraments

The trouble, he said, was that the Church of England was heir to a medieval unreformed system of bishops, who had ruled impossibly large dioceses. So that's why the present system had grown up in which a senior – or diocesan – bishop may have one or more junior or suffragan bishops to help him. But, said Dr Bennett, you cannot multiply bishops. The people of God relate to a person, not to a committee.

And the fact is that many suffragan bishops are rather con-fused about their role. Are they bishops? If they are, how is it that they are not solely responsible for one Christian com-munity, but work to a 'boss', as it were?

Well, given that the Church of England has a tendency to be

all in favour of change, provided that everything remains exactly the same, everyone knows there would be an outcry if the synod tried to split up the dioceses into smaller units. So one answer is to do what happens in some places already – that is, to have area bishops, suffragan bishops responsible for one part of the diocese, perhaps a hundred clergy. Dr Bennett reckons that's about the most one man can relate to effectively. He urged that the suffragans should be better represented in senior bishops' meetings, and that much more effective ways should be found of making sure that suffragans are really in touch with clergy and laity.

Bishops are fond of talking of their role as the focus of unity. But many people in the pews hardly know who the bishop is.

This throws an interesting sidelight on a current debate in the Church of Scotland. Some church unity proposals are feared by some people as being the thin end of a wedge whose thick end could be bishops in the kirk. The odd thing is that in Presbyterian Scotland there's still a tendency to talk about bishops as if they brought with them overtones of the medieval princes of the church, corrupted by power. In fact, as most Church of England members would tell them, that's no longer the problem at all. Most of the bishops are very nice men, worn down by a treadmill of administration. That's a much better reason for the kirk not having them.

The clarity of Dr Bennett's contribution was a bright light in a rather dim debate. For he tried to go back to first principles, and *then* to work out practically what should be done to change current practice.

It struck me this week how much of synodical debating time is spent tinkering with the wheels rather than remembering the carriage. After all, a bishop's role is not only to keep the administrative wheels going, or to look after the clergy, or to answer loopy letters. The first principle is to help people know God, love him and serve him in this world, and to be happy with him for ever in the next.

23 November 1985

Synodical Games

Here in York I'm sitting looking at the pleasant lawns of the university, the weeping willows overhanging the lakes and a family of ducks waddling down for a morning swim. Soon the 550 members of the Church of England General Synod will be making their way back into the main university hall to start debates on church fees, sanctions against South Africa, and the nature of belief. But today the main topic is whether or not to allow the 750 or so women legally ordained in Anglican churches abroad to celebrate holy communion in Church of England parishes. But even if the legalisation gets the two-thirds majority required in all three houses – bishops, lay people and clergy – the permission will be hedged around with restrictions. Before a visiting woman will be allowed to celebrate communion, she'll have to have the permission of the parish priest, the parochial church council and the bishop of the diocese concerned.

To get this far, the proposed legislation has had to survive several serious battles and various synodical manoeuvrings. One of the synod members who knows his way round the standing orders extremely well is the chairman of the business subcommittee. Yesterday Canon Brian Brindley was looking rather festive, as clergymen go, with a fawn jacket and purple socks. He was spotted the day before at the Henley regatta wearing the same outfit. But our informant, Mr Morrison from the Oxford diocese, had a more serious point to make. This was that he believed many synod members were deeply unhappy that the coming debates about women priests had been preceded for weeks by what he described as a 'storm of flag-waving' in the media by advocates and opponents of women priests alike. Such confrontation, he said, was a recipe for self-destruction. And it confused the silent majority in the church who had not bowed the knee to any petition, or kissed any list. He found it difficult to understand the strong feelings in some quarters and the great noise they were making about it all. This speech was greeted by warm applause. It was an interesting corrective to anyone who has the impression that the Church of England is split into two camps who spend the whole time at each other's throats. A great many people in the Church of England are appalled by talk of dividing up the parishes into this church and that church and splitting up the assets and working out pay-offs for clergy threatening to leave. They want to carry on worshipping quietly at their parish church and they want to be part of one church, the Church of England.

Canon Brindley's response to Mr Morrison was revealing. At Henley he said he had seen people race very hard, but still retain a sense of fair play, humour and sportsmanship. He hoped the same was true of the synod. His remark left some synod members wondering whether synodical games – even with humour and sportsmanship – were the right way to approach the government and leadership of the church.

For the fact is that a good deal of the posturing we have heard over the past months about women priests is little more than tactics in a very long, highly complicated, highly political game that makes winning Wimbledon positively straightforward. Ways of loading the dice – part of the synodical understanding of 'fair play' – include doing your utmost to try to pack committees the way you want them, giving the impression that the worst consequences seem as if they could be serious, even likely events (this ploy is in order to swing votes in your favour), putting up amendments to ensure you are called to speak, scouring standing orders for ways to delay or obstruct decisions already made. This last tactic could well be wheeled out this morning, for instance, in a debate on the ordination of women deacons.

Yesterday afternoon at the opening of the synod, the Archbishop of York led prayers for the guidance of the Holy Spirit. But watching the synod one might be forgiven for getting the impression that some people have given up on the Holy Spirit in this assembly. It is the result of a system of synodical government that disastrously imitated a secular model, and is now reaping the cost. That cost is the creation of confusion in the minds of ordinary churchgoers up and down the land, who don't understand that some of the scare stories they take seriously are merely sportsmanlike tactics in an elaborate synodical game. The truth is that the game is a dangerous one.

5 July 1986

6

ROMAN
ROADS

All Latin to Me

One of my American jounalist colleagues informs me that somewhere in the depths of the Vatican – probably at the end of a long echoing corridor – works an American Carmelite priest called the Reverend Reginald Foster. He has what must be one of the most bizarre jobs on earth. He's in charge of compiling the new Vatican edition of a Latin dictionary. As part of that job, he has to contact other Latin experts all over the world to discuss the tricky problem of translating into Latin words that did not exist when Latin was actually a living language. For instance, say you're translating into Latin a church document. And you wish to say 'I lost my toothbrush and a tape-recorder.' Not a sentence that is likely to feature often, I grant you, but it's as well to be prepared, as the Guides say. So what do you do? Well, Father Foster's dictionary should make all clear. Do not get *sollicitatur* – that, apparently, is his word for 'uptight'. If you need a toothbrush, he says, ask for a *peniculus dentarius*. A tape-recorder, *magnetophonium*. TV is much more complicated: *imaginum transmissio per electricas undas*. About 10,000 new Latin words have been concocted to boost the language's original 30,000 words or so.

Why doesn't the Vatican adopt a single modern language and have done with all this? The answer is that the Vatican increasingly *does* use modern languages, but that Latin is the

ancient and traditional form of communication, that it favours
no modern nation in particular, and that using it for certain
documents is cheaper than translating everything into many
different languages. So although Father Foster's work seems
remote, it is, say his superiors, nevertheless very useful.

Well, it struck me this week that church unity talks appear to
be in the same sort of category. They're intended to be very
useful in the end, but in the mean time they are in fact mostly
incomprehensible to the general public. This came home to me
strongly last week when the Church of England's General
Synod had a preliminary and rather nervous stab at debating
two interchurch documents – first, the final report of the Anglican-Roman Catholic International Commission, known as AR-
CIC, which saw the light of day last year after eleven years of
talks, and second, the World Council of Churches document on
baptism, the eucharist and the ministry. Both are convergent
documents, in that although there is not total agreement, a lot
of the old brambles have been cleared away. The various
churches are now in the process of examining the theologians'
work and seeing whether they approve. But it is plain that the
communications problems are immense. Let me give you an
example. The Anglican-Roman Catholic document recommended that if the two churches were ever reunited, the Bishop
of Rome should be accepted as 'universal primate'. This was
popularly feared by some people to mean that the Pope might
soon take over the Church of England. In fact the job of
universal primate, as envisaged by the ARCIC members, is not
at all the same as the job performed at present by the Pope. And
the careful choice of the words 'the Bishop of Rome' instead of
the word 'Pope' was intended to emphasise that. In the ARCIC
vision of the long-term future, the Bishop of Rome would be
accepted by his brother bishops as 'first among equals'. The
style of church government would be through consultation and
consensus.

The ARCIC team also spent many months discussing the
meaning of the eucharist. They came to remarkable agreement
on this too, but in doing so they avoided using some of the old

language that had divided the churches in the past. One of the most divisive words was 'transubstantiation' – a word used by Roman Catholics in the sixteenth century to explain how the Lord was present in the communion. As I understand it, a whole medieval philosophy lay behind that word. The philosophy was that everything had an abstract metaphysical substance, as well as a physical substance. Under the theory of transubstantiation, the metaphysical substance of the bread and wine is annihilated, and replaced by the body and blood of Christ. But what happens if you no longer believe that bread and wine *have* a metaphysical substance? That means that words like transubstantiation no longer explain *how* the Lord is present. *That*'s one of the reasons why the ARCIC theologians have tried to re-express what they believe in *new* language. No doubt the church will eventually want this new language translated back into Latin. So Father Foster could well be burning the midnight oil again in his Vatican hide-out.

23 July 1983

Roman Holiday

I've spent this week in the cool autumn sunshine of Rome. The last days of summer are still in the air, but the birds are gathering above the piazzas to fly south, and the tourists are beginning to pack their bags at the end of the season. But in St Peter's Square, you can still see visitors busy with their cameras. Among them yesterday was a group of Africans standing cheerfully on some steps ready for what looked for all the world like a school picture. Their uniform was the long black robes and red or purple waistbands and skull-caps of the fathers of the church. For these were just some of the 200 or so bishops and cardinals of the world-wide Roman Catholic Church who have been meeting for the last month at the Vatican. They've been attending the synod of bishops, a sort of parliament of the church, which comes together to advise the Pope, roughly every three years. Last time they discussed the family; this time the theme's been reconciliation and the sacrament of penance.

Now it has to be said that that doesn't sound much like a news story. And before the synod began, some cynical voices could be heard claiming that they already knew what would emerge. The bishops would say that sin was a bad thing; they would review the working of the church's three different rites regarding confession; and they would work out strategies to try to reverse the decline in the numbers of people going into the confession box. There were clear signs that this is what the Curia both wanted and expected.

Well, the publication on Thursday [27 October] of the bishops' message to the church and the world shows that their concerns have in fact ranged much wider. Published against the background of the latest developments in Grenada and the Lebanon, the bishops' message says they will try to reduce east–west tension. They call for a tireless search for peace and disarmament. They condemn all racial discrimination, all warlike aggressiveness, violence and terrorism. They also denounce the deprivation of human rights and the structures of the world whereby the rich become richer and the poor poorer.

You may feel that this message is a variation of the bishops saying they are 'against sin'. But if *they* don't have a vision of healing and reconciliation in a divided world, the church would be in a pretty poor way. Incidentally, it's something of a novelty for a message to come out of the Vatican which has not originated from the Pope. Vatican observers say it's a sign of the growing influence of Third World bishops. Certainly it was partly due to them that the synod overall refused to accept the narrowing down of the theme of reconciliation to an ecclesiastical discussion on the sacrament of penance. There was a minor rebellion. Some of the horses, although not exactly *refusing* the jumps prepared by the Curia, preferred a more open field. They started asking fundamental questions. Bishop Peter Cullinane of New Zealand pointed out the gap between the church and the way many *ordinary* people perceive it. For instance, references to the church as the 'sacrament and sign of reconciliation'. People, he said, did not always experience it like that. The danger, he implied, was an exaggerated confidence in one's own virtues.

Another bishop got up and asked what was mortal sin – an odd question for a bishop, when you think about it. But he was trying to highlight changing attitudes. Missing Mass occasionally on Sundays, for instance, no longer seemed the one-way ticket to hell it had once been. If the concept of mortal sin was changing, shouldn't they honestly face up to that and make things clearer?

A German delegate enquired how confessors should respond to people who confessed minor personal sins, but whose way of life *overall* exploited and damaged others. There was a lot of talk, too, about something called 'structural' sin, which sounded like a way of letting individuals off the hook. One Indian bishop spoke of what he saw as the sinful forces of trading patterns, international banking policies and multinationals. The bishops have accepted the notion of structural sin, while emphasising that any structure is made up of far-from-blameless individuals.

In the end synod made no decisions, though it has presented a list of suggestions to the Pope. Its main role is to be a sounding board for ideas.

Cardinal Hume turned out to be one of the most popular speakers at the synod. Speaking to journalists, he made no excuse for the breadth of the bishops' discussions, and admitted quite openly that many people who had the will to achieve change, did not have the power. Part of the bishops' future work would be to persuade people who do have the power, to summon the necessary will to get on with it.

29 October 1983

Biffing Boff

In Rome yesterday, where the weather is still warm and sunny, the trial of the Brazilian liberation theologian, Father Leonardo Boff, began and ended. It took him no more than four hours to answer immediate queries about his work from the department of the church that deals with matters of faith and morals, and today he's expected to fly home to Brazil. The meeting was apparently informal and cordial and the Vatican now says it will, on the basis of their conversation and his fifty-page written defence, examine his writings and arguments further. Speaking to reporters afterwards, Father Boff said that the theology of Rome seemed to be drawn up by Europeans who were mere spectators of the real poor of the world. The church, Father Boff went on, has a paternalistic vision. It should be in the front line with the poor, ready to live like them, starve like them, be tortured like them and, if necessary, die like them

That comment, in a nutshell, summarises the attitude of many liberation theologians. Liberation theology is intensely class-conscious and reflects a certain range of biblical references – from Moses leading the children of Israel out of captivity in Egypt, to Jesus' advice to the rich young man to sell all his goods and give the proceeds to the poor. It it also passionately Latin American – full of pain and suffering and longing. It's so rooted in the harshness of so much of Latin American life that it's no wonder that the first reaction of many people with a half-comfortable way of life in western Europe, is to shy away from it. But the fact is it won't go away. And the publication of the 10,000-word Vatican document this week warning against certain trends in liberation theology is a sign of the Vatican's recognition of its strong influence in the Third World and its potentially even greater influence if economic and social conditions worsen.

The Vatican document does not denounce liberation theology. What it does do is strongly to criticise any tendency within the different liberation theologies – for there are many – to adopt Marxist patterns of thought.

On the positive side, the Rome document reaffirms the church's commitment to a bias to the poor and it says specifically that the term 'theology of liberation' is a valid one. But the overall message is that whereas when liberation theology is good, it is very, very good, when it is bad, unless it is corrected, it might very soon become horrid. The face of horridness is Marxism and the Vatican weighs in heavily against communist smiles. It says that atheism and the denial of liberty and human rights are at the core of Marxism. And it reminds its listeners that historically many members of atheist and totalitarian regimes who talked about liberation when out of power, themselves denied millions of people their basic rights once in power.

Marxist tools are sometimes used by liberation theologians in their analysis of society. For instance, many would regard the analysis of class conflict as a help towards explaining why the poor remain poor.

But the Vatican document says that if you take only one part of Marxist analysis, the whole ideology is so unified that you end up eventually having to accept the lot. So the logical conclusion is that the gospel is secularised and the church becomes not the universal church, but the church of one class or another. Bishops who don't share the so-called 'correct' views may then be denounced as belonging to the class of the oppressors. The end of this path, says the Vatican, is atheism.

Defenders of the liberation theologians respond that the Vatican's position is itself not very logical, and they argue that the document fails to prove its basic point that if people adopt one part of Marxist thinking, they end up taking the lot. They point out that even Marxists themselves are disillusioned with some aspects of Marxist theory. They also point out that the document fails to include one word of repentance for the church's past record in Latin America when it was linked with cruel and oppressive regimes. Moreover, they say that if a peasant from Latin America were to read the document he or she would certainly know at the end of it what they should not do, but might be very little inspired or encouraged about what they could do.

The Vatican is sensitive to that last point, and is now preparing another paper giving a positive vision of liberation theology.

8 September 1984

Sin

Last Tuesday [11 December] the Pope issued a document 140 pages long on reconciliation and penance. A brief scan of any of the newspapers on the stands in St Peter's Square, Rome, shows – in Catholic eyes at any rate – how much the world *needs* repentance: stories of murder, hunger, loneliness and injustice. Yet over the last twenty years fewer and fewer Roman Catholics have made their way to the confession box. Yet at the same time, more Catholics are going to Mass. So why have so many people stopped making individual confessions? Have they lost a sense of sin? And anyway, what *is* sin these days? And what effect have all the insights of twentieth-century psychology had? These are some of the subjects the Pope grapples with in the document.

The document itself is the longest to be issued by a pope this century. Through a hiccup in communication channels, only a few copies are available in England. But printed extracts of the document bear as usual the marks of Vaticanese. The extracts are complex, philosophical, and at times difficult to read. Though the document reflects discussions on the subject by 200 bishops from all over the world, who met in Rome in the autumn of 1983, nevertheless the broad outline seems to fit in with what are generally accepted as the views of the Curia on the subject. But it also bears strong signs of the Pope's own personality – his passionate commitment to evangelisation and conversion, meaning a radical change of heart, and his insistence that sin can never exclude personal responsibility. The Pope is convinced that the world's foundations are being shattered by people's loss of a sense of sin, and he declares that a personal meeting between priest and sinner in private confession must remain the prime method of confession. *General* absolution by which a large number of people can receive forgiveness for their sins at a special service is not, he says, on the whole acceptable to the church.

Of course, as long as most of us can remember, priests, bishops and popes have been lamenting the loss of a sense of sin. But a number of bishops at the synod in Rome spoke of confusion among ordinary Catholics about what was or was not considered a sin these days. Whereas missing Mass on Sundays was once considered a mortal sin, for instance, these days some priests speak of mortal sin as something that happens perhaps only two or three times in the lifetime of most Catholics.

In traditional Roman Catholic teaching, sin can be either venial or mortal. The difference is basic. Imagine that the journey towards God is like being on a fast train to Edinburgh. If we decide to get off that train and go somewhere completely different, that's mortal sin. But what if out of laziness or curiosity we get off and take a number of slower trains going a roundabout way? Basically we are still going to Edinburgh, so the detour is a venial sin. Quite different from getting off and deciding, freely and consciously, not to go to Edinburgh at all. But the Pope warns that mortal sin must not be reduced to rejecting God in sins like idolatry or atheism. It is also, he says, in every act of disobedience to God's commandments in a grave matter.

But don't some people start their moral lives with an inborn disadvantage? Say, for instance, that in your early life you never had an experience of being loved or treated with dignity. Well, the Pope believes that some forms of modern psychology, in their aim to avoid creating feelings of guilt, or limits on freedom, have led people to refuse to admit any shortcomings, preferring instead to blame society and not themselves. The Pope agrees that the individual may be conditioned and influenced by many external factors, and he discusses the concept of so-called 'social sin' in some depth. But he insists that none of the meanings of social sin excludes personal responsibility. To deny personal responsibility, he says, is to deny the Christian belief in human freedom.

The Pope lists illustrations of sin – among them violations of human rights, racial discrimination, torture, the arms race and the unjust distribution of wealth. But he detects a widespread desire for reconciliation. And then he goes on to speak of the church's role in bringing about a radical change of heart. The document emphasises without compromise the value of church discipline in the celebration of the sacraments. For against the seriousness of sin, the Pope puts the saving power of God. Through prayer and the sacraments, the church must first work to reconcile divisions within itself, and then to reconcile the world.

The Pope, it seems, is holding the guiding reins of the Roman Catholic Church firmly.

15 December 1984

The Pope Flies in

In the next hour or so, Pope John Paul II should be boarding an aeroplane in Rome for the start of another of his visits to his parishioners around the world. This time the aeroplane points through the clouds to Venezuela, Ecuador and Peru.

Some years ago I spent seven weeks travelling by bumpy bus around that part of Latin America. I can remember now the green banana plantations of Ecuador and the raunchy humid port of Guayaquil, followed by Peru's long dry dusty desert along the Pacific, where phosphorescence makes the sea glow and twinkle at night. After that there were the wealthy suburbs of Lima, the capital of Peru, where the generals lived, and the shanty towns around the edge of the city where there's no running water.

From Lima, you can get a train up to the towering Andes. They serve spicy food on the train, and the track goes so high the conductor has to come round in a white coat offering oxygen. And then you can take a bus travelling if you wish by moonlight through the narrow winding roads of the mountains, on to Cuzco, the ancient Inca capital. The air is so thin there, you feel dizzy when you arrive. It's to these and other places the Pope will go in the next twelve days.

As usual the Pope will be talking to a range of people – steel workers, presidents and politicians, priests and businessmen, Indians and shanty-town dwellers. He may even be heard by revolutionaries. In Peru, he will stop briefly at Ayacucho, a town which will be stiff with security men. I was stranded there for two days and sold a shirt to pay for my hotel. Today it's a centre of guerrilla operations by a group which calls itself Sendero Luminoso, or Shining Light. About 400 people are said to have died in the area since 1980, many of them in Indian village massacres. At the airport, Andean peasants have been ordered not to wear their traditional, brilliantly coloured ponchos, which could conceal bombs. The President of Peru hopes the Pope's visit will end the violence.

Peru is, of course, one of the homes of liberation theology – the theology which commits the church to a bias towards the poor and suffering, and which is sometimes described as if one of its main effects was to justify revolutionary violence. In fact, it has no more to do with violence than the traditional theology which developed the theory of a just war, which has for centuries been used to justify Christians killing people. But liberation theology *is* a reaction to the fatalism of much popular religion in Latin America.

One of the things that struck me profoundly as I travelled around Latin America was the style of the churches. In Quito, for instance, the capital of Ecuador, while *outside* the church doors you may see people clustered in the markets evidently living in extreme poverty, *inside* are solid gold altars. But more to the point is the style of the art inside the church. Around the walls are hung agonising pictures of the crucifixion. I suppose somewhere I must have seen a portrayal of resurrection – of glowing light and hope – but I can't recall it. To liberation theologians, a Jesus who only suffers is not liberating – and one of the aims of *early* liberation theology was to challenge this popular cult of suffering and fatalism. *Later* the theologians began to believe that instead of teaching the poor, they needed first to *learn* from the poor.

But the Vatican document on liberation theology published last autumn warned against any tendency in liberation theology to take on board Marxist forms of analysis.

The message of the Pope this week is likely to be in essence what he told the Peruvian bishops when they visited Rome last October. It was both a stimulus and a warning. To those who were doing little to try to change the status quo, he gave a reminder that it was their duty to be reconcilers in society and to try to create a new order in which the rights of men and women are promoted. All pastors, he said, must work seriously in the cause of justice and the defence of the poor. To others he warned that this work must never be done in a way that empha-sises class divisions or reduces the gospel to a materialist philos-ophy. Nor should it create dissension in the church. Instead it must be in a spirit of unity with the bishops and the Pope himself. For the Pope, as for the theologians, liberation means freedom. But not freedom to do what you like at any cost to anyone else. The Pope would say it's liberation from sin – your own and other people's.

26 January 1985

Red Hats

As you may have seen, the Pope this week has been handing out red hats. Twenty-eight new cardinals from nineteen countries will soon be sporting new headgear, including for the first time men from Marxist Ethiopia and left-wing Nicaragua. There's also a new strongly pro-Solidarity cardinal in Poland. There's been some comment about how this latest list of promotions reflects the Pope's continuing determination to make the college of cardinals more international. That's certainly true. But Italians still hold a large slice of the cake. The appointment now of a further five Italian cardinals – making that country's score up to thirty-five – means that Italians account for nearly a quarter of all cardinals.

What's more interesting is to mull through this latest selection and see who and what is in the Pope's favour and what message this signals to the church at large. After all the Pope doesn't *have* to appoint any new cardinals at all. Indeed you might think that being a cardinal is not much different from being an archbishop, except that every once in a while you are called to Rome to help elect a new Pope. Of course there is an upgrading of prestige. (Not that new cardinals are supposed to value *that*.) But they are well aware that in the eyes of the world at least, and indeed in the ranks of their own church, the title cardinal does carry more clout than that of a mere archbishop.

So the appointment of new cardinals is the Vatican equivalent of the Queen's honours list – it's the method by which the Pope exercises his papal power and patronage, rewards the good and withholds favour from those who have displeased him.

In the list are several appointments expected as a matter of course – for instance, promotions for new heads of Vatican departments and also for archbishops of particular sees which have traditionally been led by cardinals. Among these is the see of New York. And sure enough, Archbishop John O'Connor of New York becomes, as from this week, Cardinal O'Connor. During last year's American presidential election campaign, Archbishop O'Connor was outspoken in his criticism of the 'right to choose' stand taken on abortion by the Democrat vice-presidential candidate, Congresswoman Geraldine Ferraro. Archbishop Bernard Law of Boston had joined Archbishop O'Connor in entering the political fray regarding abortion. He too has been made a cardinal this week.

In Central America, *two* archbishops were thought to be in the running for red hats: Archbishop Rivera y Damas of El Salvador, who succeeded the murdered Archbishop Romero, and Archbishop Obando y Bravo of Nicaragua, who has come into conflict with the left-wing government there, and wants them to negotiate with opposition forces. The Pope has promoted the Nicaraguan bishop only. The promotion will almost certainly have been intended to give him more weight and prestige in his relations with the government, but it will probably be interpreted by the government as a further sign of the Pope's lack of sympathy with the Sandinista revolution.

The ecclesiastical corridors in Rome of course have been full of gossip about the new appointments. But they do seem to follow a pattern which the present Pope is treading slowly and confidently during his years as supreme pontiff.

Not all the Pope's honours this time have been awarded to men generally regarded as theologically and politically conservative. There is a range, but the weight of promotion does lie in the direction you might expect from this Pope. Incidentally the appointment of another Polish cardinal brings the total number of Poles in the college of cardinals now to five – more, I am told, than ever before.

In Holland the Pope has promoted Adrianus Simonis, Archbishop of Utrecht. He's one of a series of conservative bishops the Pope has been appointing in the hope of bringing under control what he sees as the excesses of the liberal wing of the Dutch church since the Second Vatican Council in the 1960s. In two weeks' time, the Pope begins a visit to the Netherlands.

A recent poll among a thousand Roman Catholics indicated that nearly three-quarters don't want him to come. But more about Holland in due course.

27 April 1985

Solomon's Temple

I was saying last week that if I were led blindfold into a Christian assembly, I would soon know where I was because of the style of jokes. The Roman Catholic synod of bishops, having an extra meeting in Rome this week, isn't exactly renowned for its humour, even in Latin. But outside the formal meetings, jokes fly around thick and fast as autumn leaves.

Whereas Anglican jokes are often about historical church–state tensions, Catholic ones are usually a send-up of some wonderful piece of ecclesiastical non-communication. For instance, let me tell you the true story of a Catholic journalist reporting from Rome the election in 1978 of the present Pope. Before the conclave began, he asked a number of cardinals what qualities were needed for the man who would lead the church into the last years of the twentieth century. Nearly all the cardinals said that first and foremost, he must be 'a man of prayer'. After some time the journalist began asking the cardinals how many of the present college of cardinals that reply excluded. The comments of their eminences are unfortunately not recorded.

In Rome this week the same signs of non-communication continue to abound. Journalists are still not allowed to sit in on the discussions. The problems of the reporting are reflected in the strangeness of some of the write-ups emerging. But let me set the scene.

The leaders of bishops' conferences around the world are meeting to review the effects of the Second Vatican Council – the most significant event in the life of the Roman Catholic

Church this century. Since the council met in the early 1960s, the church has changed rapidly. Twenty years ago the Mass was celebrated in Latin by a priest who turned his back on the people. Now it's in the language of the congregation and the priest faces the people. The council brought with it a new openness to the world, a more sympathetic relationship with Christians of other denominations and people of other faiths, and a renewed commitment to the poor. It has also been followed by divisions in the church.

Well, for some weeks preceding the synod, some foreign newspapers built up the picture of a synod much feared in advance as a papal plot sprung to confront the more liberal bishops and to hijack the church back to the nineteenth century. This Machiavellian scenario is delightfully entertaining. Unfortunately it is also wrong.

And so now the same newspapers are beginning to write the story that for some unaccountable reason, the synod is turning out to be a *celebration* of the council. Although the bishops are discussing some errors and abuses due to misinterpretations, they are also talking about how the council can be better implemented.

The Pope's view seems to be that the divisions in the church have largely been caused by people going *beyond* the council documents, or by imposing changes too quickly without making sure they were properly understood. His own view of the papal office having supreme universal power in the church is not something that this Polish cardinal dreamed up in Cracow. It was reaffirmed by the Second Vatican Council long before he became Pope. True, the council did go on to suggest the development of a partnership between Pope and bishops. But the synod is purely consultative, cannot act independently and may be quite disregarded by the Pope if he so chooses. That is what the Second Vatican Council said.

Most bishops say the key change introduced by the council was in their understanding of the church. In the words of Cardinal Basil Hume, President of the European Conference of Bishops, the image the church has of itself nowadays is no longer that of Solomon's temple, massively fortified, set four-square against the secular world, rich in beauty and furnishings. It's rather the image of Abraham's tent, because the whole church – like the patriarch of old – is on the move through the centuries. It is making a pilgrimage of faith, searching for God in all the happenings of history.

But the symbols of Rome aren't always very helpful in communicating that idea. There's still a great deal of Solomon's temple around, whether or not the Vatican has a deficit of £35 million.

Last Sunday, the Pope and the bishops, dressed in white robes and mitres, processed formally across St Peter's Square. It was an echo of the procession for the Mass opening the council itself. If that's the sort of gear they still dress in for Abraham's tent, there may be a few minor difficulties.

30 November 1985

Set My People Free

As you may have heard, the Vatican last weekend [5–6 April] published a major document on the whole question of freedom and human rights. It was the long-awaited sequel to the much-debated 1984 instruction which had criticised any tendencies in the various forms of liberation theology towards Marxist thinking.

Whereas the tone of the first document resembled a flashing red light warning of an obstacle on the road ahead, the new publication has a different mood. It still has the feel of a driving instructor, leading a pupil whose driving ability tends to be erratic. But the signs are that the instructor this time has at least chosen the right road and pointed the car in the right direction. The road he has called Liberty Avenue.

Ever since the exodus of the people of Israel from Egypt, God's words, 'Let my people go free', have echoed through the Jewish and Christian imagination. But freedom from what?

And freedom *for* what? Does freedom have any constraints? How can it best be used? These are the questions the new Vatican instruction asks and tries to answer.

If all this sounds very philosophical, then let me say at once that it *is* very philosophical. Though the document is published by the Sacred Congregation for the Doctrine of the Faith, the Pope's hand and passion for philosophy can be detected at regular intervals.

It is ordinary Christians – not only in places like Latin America and Africa, but here at home – who can decide whether this document becomes yet another abstract set of principles gathering dust on a shelf, or whether its ideals are truly lived out.

First of all, it roots freedom in what Christ has offered to mankind through his death and resurrection. Freedom, the document suggests, is being able to do what is truly good for each other, as Christ did for us. So, in the *Christian* understanding, true freedom can never be the freedom to behave selfishly. Nor – and here the Vatican renews its criticisms of Marxism – is it just freedom from economic ills. Of course Christians should work to improve economic conditions. But liberation from material poverty, the document emphasises, does not *produce* freedom; it provides better conditions in which freedom can flourish. In other words the driving instructor is warning the driver not to get too obsessed with reaching the town in sight at the end of the road. That may be a very nice place with comfortable beds. But the real aim of the journey is an amazing city beyond that, where real love lives.

The document warns against various roads that lead away from this city. Class struggle is one of these roads. So is the 'myth of revolution'. Those who discredit the path of reform, and favour the myth of revolution, the Vatican says, not only foster the illusion that the abolition of an evil situation is in itself sufficient to create a more humane society. But they also encourage the setting-up of totalitarian regimes. The document says that in extreme cases, taking up arms as a last resort may be admissible. But it says passive resistance is a better way. The recent transformation in the Philippines is seen as an illustration of the way Christians and others *can* effect change without violence.

But the document warns against other roads too, in particular the road of unrestrained capitalism and mass unemployment. Here it restates the principles contained in the Pope's encyclical on work, '*Laborem Exercens*'. And here it speaks most sharply to the Britain we know today. Every person, it says, has a right to work. The fact that unemployment keeps large sectors of the population and notably the young on the edges of society is, it says, 'intolerable'. For this reason, job creation should be a priority of individuals and private enterprises, as well as the state. The purpose of work is to help individuals express their personality as best they can for the common good. It does not depend on the kind of work done. Practically any seriously handicapped person in Britain who has spent time looking for work in our society will know how far off *that* ideal is.

12 April 1986

7

DISSENTERS

Sizing Up Sects

Next month in the halls of power in Brussels, the European Parliament is likely to debate a set of guidelines for religious cults. And the kinds of question that will be discussed will be whether family and friends have the right to see a cult member at any time, and whether all religious movements should clearly identify themselves when out recruiting new members.

It's an area which is a religious minefield. Many parents whose children join such groups go through the shock/horror syndrome of 'I've given my children everything, why have they done this to me?' And general fear and ignorance of many of these groups have been intensified by sensational media coverage. But underlying it all is a very important question of religious freedom. And that's one reason why the proposed guidelines *are* but guidelines and *not* proposed legal requirements.

Of course the words 'sect' and 'cult' have themselves become 'boo' words – a fact members of such groups are all too aware of. The Scientologists, for instance, particularly dislike being called a 'cult'. They occasionally ring me up to detail some latest small victory in their long-running campaign to be regarded as a religion. Religion, after all, is respectable. It means, according to the *Oxford English Dictionary*, 'being one of the prevalent systems of faith and worship'.

On those grounds, I certainly regard Scientology as still a cult. And one of my definitions of a cult would be an organisation, not well integrated into society as a whole, that surrounds a charismatic figure. In the case of the Scientologists, the figure would be Mr Ron Hubbard. When I visited their centre in East Grinstead some years ago, I was shown round his old study there as if it were a sanctuary.

A sect is similar, but a bit different. There's a stronger tendency for its members to turn their faces against the world. This leads towards separatism – even, at times, to secrecy. They usually think they are the only ones who are right. A colleague of mine in religious broadcasting tells me that years ago he once received three leaflets in the same week: one from the Christadelphians, one from Christian Scientists and one from Jehovah's Witnesses. All three began with more or less the same words: 'Christendom is astray.' All three thought they had the only solution.

Sects tend to have doctrines that resemble some of the beliefs of mainstream religions, but skew them in certain directions. They also frequently come and go in the course of a single generation. But some, like the Elim Pentecostals, for instance, which began as a sect, get established, and gradually become a denomination – with Bible schools, official pastors, etc.

In fact it's quite possible to make a reasonably good case that early Christianity was a Jewish sect. The point I'm making is that the title 'sect' is not an automatic guarantee of appalling evil. Some sects, it's true, do go crazy – Jim Jones's sect that ended in the suicides in Guyana is one that did, tragically. But others don't. And people join such groups for all sorts of reasons: spiritual search, longing for companionship, a structure to organise their life and so on. I'm not sure that I find the Reverend Sun Myung Moon's activities and political links very appealing. But there is – I hear – quite a little industry among PhD students these days, exploring seriously the theology of Moon's Unification Church. Maybe one reason why people get specially nervous about the Moonies is because, as one person put it, their theology is not beyond the pale, but *at* the pale, and therefore close enough to be threatening to traditional Christianity.

Earlier this week I was sent a newsletter from one of the three main organisations that provide information about the sects and cults in Britain. It quoted an article from a student newspaper which alleged that every day Moonies approach students outside Imperial College, talk of world affairs and then invite them to their centre for a meal. What follows is a three-hour video based on the life and work of Moon. Good heavens. Members of the Unification Church actually want to *talk* to people. And even show students a *video*. A video nastie perhaps? There's a parable of Jesus' about straining out a gnat, but swallowing a camel. And there's the old saying about using a sledgehammer to crack a nut. Maybe what we really need to do is to put the sects and cults in perspective.

10 March 1984

Dissidents

Last Tuesday evening in Eastbourne, a minister of a large Baptist church in Bloomsbury got up before a crowd of people and asked himself and them the question: was he the minister of a living fellowship of the People of God? Or was he just the curator of a museum?

He was really questioning whether the Free Churches any longer had much of a future. And when you consider that between 1970 and 1980 membership of the Methodist Church declined by 20 per cent and that some other Free Churches also declined at the rate of 1 or 2 per cent a year, though numbers are steadying now, it seems like a reasonable point to make. Especially to a group of 400 delegates of the Free Church Federal Council, a body which is not exactly renowned for its youthful vitality, although it contains some battle-scarred Christian warriors.

The speaker was Dr Howard Williams, an energetic and radical Welshman, who has been elected this year's Moderator. He was urging them to resist the siren voices of other denominations calling softly 'unity, unity', beckoning them on to what could be the rocks. He was reasonably confident that there was not going to be a United Free Church of England, and he hoped they were not going to get Baptist bishops.

The Protestant Free Churches should resist anyone half-heartedly offering them do-it-yourself, construct-your-own-bishop kits. They should also resist the pressures of journalists like me who know an archbishop when they see one, but who suspect that a moderator of a church assembly isn't much of a spokesman when he's only just had time to get the feel of it before he's democratically replaced by somebody else.

It's no good, says Dr Williams, presenting a bogus unity to keep up appearances or merely to impress. The Free Churches should get on with standing for the principles they had always stood for – among them the duty of dissent. Dissent stands by the freedom to divide and differ.

What do you do, if you are stuck in your dissent? How does that match with reconciliation? If dissent means for you that Protestants hate Catholics and both despise all other faiths? Or if you are the evangelist Luis Palau and believe most people are consigned to hell? Well, Dr Williams says, dissenting understanding of the faith always speaks of the individual in relation to *others*, not in terms of an individual bleating about God and his or her own private soul. Moreover, the truth of dissent is in what it *asserts* rather than what it denies. The only two seeds of dissent which have ever taken root are love of the gospel and freedom.

Dr Williams ended by saying that what is needed is not a self-conscious Free Churchmanship in which Free Church people try to hold their own with Anglicans and Roman Catholics. Instead what's needed is what he called 'a careless and hazardous anonymity in which we care nothing about who gets the rewards as long as the work is done'. And as an illustration of a magnificent dissenter who has got it right, he cites Bishop

Desmond Tutu of South Africa. Desmond Tutu, of course, happens to be an Anglican.

I found Dr Williams's address a timely one. I detect the shadow of a tendency these days among some Anglicans in England at least to think that if they wait long enough, the Free Churches will have to unite with them in the end, because of falling numbers.

And maybe it's important that some Christians remain outside the establishment, to offer the Church of England and the Presbyterian churches of Scotland and Ireland a different understanding at times of what the Christian gospel implies. Then there's the valuable Free Church tradition of biblical exposition and teaching.

The Latin root of the word Protestant means, after all, not to protest, but to bear witness, to declare in public.

Recently, a friend told me a story about her father, who years ago was a Congregational minister in a part of Liverpool where tensions remained fairly strong between Catholic and Protestant. One day he received a formal request at a church meeting to preach a series of sermons against Roman Catholicism. It was, she said, one of the few times she saw him angry. He stood up slowly and said that his task was not to preach against any other part of the Christian church whose members followed the same Lord. His task was to preach the word in his church, and this he would continue to do. A true dissenter.

24 March 1984

Happy Returns

The tourist season here in London is now well under way with foreigners at crossroads puzzling over maps and taxi drivers trying to dodge round the back streets to avoid the traffic jams. Today everything will be even more congested as hordes of people arrive for the Wembley Cup Final. Among the travellers arriving last night from all round the country were over 10,000 young people dressed in green and yellow.

Many of them will have their hair dyed in those colours –
splashed with food dye, poster paint or hair spray and then
sprinkled with glitter and tinsel. Some will have their jeans
dyed green and yellow too. No, not the colours of Everton or
Manchester United. But the colours of the Methodist Association of Youth Clubs. For these particular visitors, aged between thirteen and twenty-five, are here not for the Cup Final,
though many are football fans, but to celebrate the fortieth
birthday party of the association, which has happened to clash
with the final. And they're bringing hundreds of square birthday cakes ready to assemble them all together at ten o'clock this
morning into one huge patchwork cake. Instant decorating via
icing packs will challenge everyone's creative flair, presuming,
of course, that the cakes haven't by then been reduced to
crumbs.

The association, or MAYC as it's known, is well used to
organising big annual jamborees, although *this* weekend is the
biggest they've ever had. Its purpose is first and foremost to
celebrate shared faith. But alongside the anniversary services at
the Royal Albert Hall are a host of other events, including a rock
music festival in Brixton, complete with twelve breakdancers
from East Ham called 'The Fresh Rockers', an evening of
drama, music and dance at the Methodist headquarters in
Westminster and a huge show tonight at the Royal Albert Hall,
with a cast of – well, if not thousands, certainly *a* thousand.

Somehow I doubt whether the dressing-rooms will be large
enough. But who cares? Not they. The corridors will probably
do just as well. The show will feature giant caterpillars, the
MAYC orchestra and singers, robotic chickens and a skit on the
BBC with the Director-General being played by Basil Brush.

Where, you may wonder, do all these people sleep? The
answer is in church halls, private homes and wherever they can
fit in. Not that sleep is a very high priority this weekend.

Most of the 5,000 who travelled down for the first MAYC
London weekend in 1945 slept in air-raid shelters.

The founder and inspirer of it all was the Reverend Douglas

Griffiths, known universally in Methodist circles as 'Griff'. To begin with, the powers-that-be in the Methodist Church refused to back him, saying that such a scheme would never get off the ground. So he started the first London weekend out of his own pocket, even risking hiring the Albert Hall. In those early days, the mood was rather more sober – suits and gymnastics being in vogue. But Douglas Griffiths was determined to do something about the lack of provision for young people just after the war, specially those just being demobbed from the services. Forty years on, his work is still going strong.

The different Christian denominations are well aware that the age of fifteen or sixteen is an important period for shifting attitudes about Christianity. The results of the recent evangelistic campaign to London by the Argentine/American evangelist Luis Palau indicate that young people under twenty-five, already loosely connected with churches, are the ripest field for evangelism. But research also shows many teenagers of that age have a seriously deteriorating view of Christianity. For many of them, attitudes formed at this age persist into adult life.

MAYC is one attempt to help teenagers get through that period of intellectual and spiritual searching. The London weekend is the highspot of the year, yet the hardest work is done week in week out at hundreds of groups in the various Methodist circuits. They offer Bible study groups, youth centres, even unemployment projects, in a number of full-time centres in major cities. Their success or failure depends, as usual, very much on the character and enthusiasm of the local leader.

These days there's more talk than there used to be about the participation of young people in church assemblies, even though the signs are that most young people aren't really that interested. This morning at Westminster Theatre MAYC has organised an informal debate on participation, one of the themes of International Youth Year. Less than 4 per cent of the young Methodists crowding into London this weekend are expected to attend. I bet far more will be there for the rock concert and the worship.

18 May 1985

House Church Holiday

Who would spend a week of their summer holiday camping in a cowshed surrounded by 5,500 other people in caravans and tents on a wet showground? The answer is quite a lot of people – Christian families who this week were flooded out of their tents in Harrogate showground during the tenth annual meeting of the Dales Bible Week. The animal sheds with their corrugated roofs and concrete floors had been cleaned out recently after the Yorkshire Show, but it was still fairly spartan living.

But there seemed to be no dampening of spirits. In spare moments, children rushed around squirting each other with water pistols and playing football with their parents. I even saw a jogger. But the *purpose* of the week was to get together with Christians from all over Britain and even abroad, to worship, to study the Bible and to have a good time. In some cases group solidarity was so strong that almost the entire congregation of a local church had turned up. Surprising? Yes. But not so surprising when you know that nearly all came from the independent house church movement.

That's the movement which has mushroomed over the last twenty years as a reaction to what its members regard as the spiritual deadness of many of the mainline denominational churches. Its characteristics include intense seriousness about faith and a strong commitment to other Christians in their fellowships. The fellowships are strengthened and united by a hierarchy of relationships, in which children submit in love to their parents, wives to husbands, husbands to those called apostles, apostles to leaders and leaders to God. You may find that comforting or threatening, depending on your point of view. If the leaders think a visit to the Dales Bible Week is a good thing, most of the congregations cheerfully start packing ready to take part.

A day spent wandering around provided me with some serious food for thought. For there's no doubt about it, the house church movement displays great strengths in areas where the other churches are most vulnerable. The most obvious is its attractiveness to young people, who seemed to be having a marvellous time. For a start they like the worship – the catchiness of the songs, the freedom to clap and dance, the nineteen-piece orchestra with piano, guitars, violinists and lead singers. They like the singing in tongues and the semi-mystical mood it can induce in the congregation. But as well as that, they like the preaching. On Wednesday night, without fidgeting they sat silently through an address which lasted not five minutes, or half-an-hour, or even an hour. It lasted no less than an hour and a half. At the end of it, about 1,000 people, most of them young, flocked up to the platform, as a sign of their commitment to spread the gospel. The theme of the preaching was that Britain was on the edge of a great spiritual revival, that the kingdom of God *is* coming, and that they need to be young John the Baptists *in this age*.

Of course some of the main-line churches do organise youth meetings and Bible studies. The Methodist Association of Youth Clubs, for instance, has some very lively branches. And evangelicals organise huge meetings like Spring Harvest in Prestatyn. But statistics suggest that the traditional churches have a credibility problem with many young people after a certain age. Faith often declines sharply through the teenage years.

People sometimes complain that the churches don't talk to them enough about where they are in their lives. But part of the success of the house church style of teaching seems to be that it is rooted in everyday life. Seminar leaders talk openly about marriage difficulties and their own experiences of how Christian couples can help each other with the aid of the fellowship. At one seminar, the sister-in-law of Bryn Jones, the leader of the Bradford house church, was talking about healing. She believes that many, many people have been healed through the prayers of Christians, yet her youngest son has not been healed of a severe chest complaint. She spoke honestly and openly about the pressures that had been put on her faith and how she has come to realise and slowly accept that though God answers prayers, his answers are not always the ones Christians expect.

There's not always very much love lost between the house churches and the traditional denominations, who sometimes feel the house churches have poached their congregations. At the Dales Bible Week, I sometimes encountered a holier than thou attitude to other Christians, and an unwillingness to recognise the many different paths to God. But it seems the house churches are responding to a real hunger, where people in our impersonal age want more than can be given during an occasional hour in church on a Sunday.

3 August 1985

Christmas Cracker

If on Christmas Day you drive past the rather grand headquarters in North London of the Jehovah's Witnesses, you will see the hundred or so unpaid staff quietly working away at their desks, just as if it's any old day. There'll be no Christmas trees, no mince pies, no office parties, and not a single Christmas card anywhere to be seen. It's a scene that should appeal to the artist of a Christmas card I saw this week which showed a couple sitting at home with deeply satisfied smiles on their faces. The date on the calendar on the mantelpiece is 27 December. Their living room is completely cleared of all reminders of Christmas. Instead all the presents and cards and wrapping paper and decorations are piled on the roaring log fire.

The movement known as Jehovah's Witnesses began life in the United States in the nineteenth century. Witnesses are renowned for their rejection of military service, their refusal to salute a national flag or to offer allegiance to any sovereign other than Jehovah. They believe that the end of the world is nigh, though *how* nigh is a matter of dispute. Some years ago the leadership declared that the final battle between God and Satan at Armageddon would take place in 1975. But anyway the movement still has 3 million or so followers world-wide – and is currently growing at the rate of 7 per cent a year. But no Jehovah's Witnesses, whether Russians, Koreans or Scots, celebrate Christmas.

In the early days of the movement, this was not so. It wasn't till the 1920s that Witnesses became increasingly uncomfortable about Christmas.

The main reason is that the odds against Christ having been born on 25 December are more than 365 to 1. The date was chosen rather arbitrarily by a pope in the year 350. It coincided with a pagan celebration sacred to Altis, a sun god, and to Mithras, the god of light, much worshipped by Roman soldiers. By choosing the same date, the early Christians were trying to make a stand against that pagan – and finally dissolute – festival. If the story of the shepherds is taken seriously, then the winter date becomes even more suspect. One biblical scholar, Jim Fleming, who lectures at the Hebrew University in Jerusalem, has recently argued that shepherds in those days were not allowed in the fields after the ground was ploughed in October and November, to allow the winter rains to soak into the parched earth. On the other hand, they *were* encouraged to allow their sheep to graze in the late summer and early autumn in order to eat the stubble of sown crops and fertilise the fields.

So the day we celebrate has no historical basis and all those carols about the bleak midwinter are historically questionable, though they may contain profound theological truths. The year of Christ's birth is also in question. Jim Fleming suggests that the year Christ was born was as early as 12 BC and the star was Halley's comet, turning up on one of its 2,300 appearances in the earth's skies. But other scholars think that 7 BC is a more likely date, because three times during that year the planets Jupiter and Saturn appeared to come together.

But Jehovah's Witnesses have other problems with Christmas, as well as the dating difficulty. They feel Christ's name has been besmirched with all associations of commercialism, excessive eating, drinking and revelry. In the seventeenth century the Puritans felt much the same. In 1647 the Puritans, who had then taken over the government of Britain, actually *banned* Christmas. Their attitude was summed up by one Hezekiah Woodward who denounced Christmas as the 'good old heathen's feasting day, the profane man's ranting day, the superstitious man's idol day, and Satan's working day'.

For many Christians, of course, the *date* of Christmas, apart from the pleasure of tradition, is neither here nor there. What matters is the celebration and the memory of the birth of a redeemer. Some Christians would like to see the church cut loose from all the razzmatazz of the secular Christmas and in fact desert 25 December. Instead, they argue, western Christians should join some Christians of the eastern world in celebrating Christmas on 7 January. Such Christians as the Russian Orthodox, the Ukrainian Catholics, the Egyptian Copts, the Ethiopians and those Greeks who follow the ancient calendar. The date of Christmas has long been in dispute between western and some eastern churches. This could be a way of resolving it. But the chances at present are as remote as my going to the moon. So, for another year, a happy 25 December.

21 December 1985

America Ahoy!

This afternoon thousands of people will be gathering among the pigeons in Trafalgar Square for yet another demonstration. But this time, the demo is for Jesus Christ. A rally launches the start of a seven-week evangelistic campaign in London by the Argentine-born evangelist, Luis Palau.

What Nelson at the top of his column will think of this foreigner taking over the square is open to question. John Ryan, the gentle cartoonist on the *Catholic Herald*, and creator of

Captain Pugwash, has pictured Nelson giving quiet orders to the pigeons as to what should go slap in the eye of the Argentine evangelist.

But I'm sure Dr Palau can cope with a great deal more than that. Certainly at a press conference at a London hotel yesterday, he looked fit and well – younger than his forty-eight years. His enthusiasm for evangelising is evident, and he certainly has a great deal of experience to fall back on. The publicity director of his campaign works occasionally for Mrs Thatcher on Tory conferences. The publicity hand-outs say Dr Palau has preached in person now to more that 5 million people in thirty-seven nations. Listeners in Scotland will know him through his campaign in Glasgow in 1981, preaching to 200,000 people. Last year he spent ten days evangelising in Leeds. Two of his radio programmes are said to be heard daily by 15 million in twenty Spanish-speaking countries.

In fact, he left Argentina twenty-three years ago, and is an American citizen. His style is the punchy, buoyant, American evangelical style. But he dismisses as 'intellectual laziness' criticism that the campaign is American razzmatazz. His whole aim, he says, is for all London to hear the voice of God. He's dreamed about it for twenty years, but his 'Mission to London' has been organised not by Americans but by British people. One thousand London churches, 40 per cent of them Church of England, the rest Protestants ranging from Baptists to Pentecostals, are closely involved. But in any case, what's the matter with American things? We have American cars, movies, missiles, Dr Palau said, why not other things too?

He dismisses accusations that evangelical campaigns of this nature only touch the already committed, and destroy the continuing evangelistic work of the churches. As to suggestions that the results don't last, he says that 85 per cent of the people converted in Leeds last year are still following Christ.

Well, you may be thinking, why is there a need for yet another evangelistic campaign? Dr Palau says that one good reason is that the commander-in-chief has ordered it. Not that he thinks God has outlined all the *particular* details of this campaign, down to the ordering of the tents, or such like. He has in mind the general commandment to spread the word and the hope of eternal life. Next, Dr Palau believes that the west is becoming peopled with intellectual giants and moral pygmies. It desperately needs a moral revival if we are not all to 'go back to the jungle'. He points out that 90 per cent or so of Londoners do not go to church regularly, if at all, and that some children these days are being raised almost totally ignorant of the Bible and its stories.

Many of his views would be wholeheartedly supported by the man he described as his elder brother, Dr Billy Graham, who is also coming to Britain soon, to campaign not for Mission London, but for Mission England. Dr Graham has asked that at least half of the members of the regional organising committees should be aged under forty. That campaign is very securely based in the local churches who are spending months and months preparing the ground. Dr Palau was keen to dispel any notion of rivalry between his and Dr Graham's coming campaign.

Dr Palau was asked his view on the right-wing Moral Majority movement in America. His response was cagey. He was not a member, he said, nor was he familiar with all they were up to. He gave the impression of general, though not total, sympathy. He was also asked about his commitment to what his publicity material calls his ministry to 'top national leadership'. Yes, he said, it was important to try to reach everyone. Would that mean visits to Number Ten and Buckingham Palace? he was asked. He said he hadn't been invited. But he was praying about it.

3 September 1983

Mormon Musings

In what used to be called the Wild West – that landscape of wide plains, rugged mountains and blue skies – a new type of traveller arrives these days. Take Salt Lake City, for instance, in Utah, the prosperous home of the Church of Jesus Christ of Latter Day Saints, better known as the Mormons. Its first inhabitants arrived one hot July in 1847, tired and dusty after a trek of 1,000 miles or so, many from Illinois and Missouri. They were pulling hand-carts with their belongings piled high – pots and pans, clothes, children, axes and all the other basics needed for starting a new life where they could practise their religion freely. Legend has it that their prophet and leader, Brigham Young, stood on the pass on the Wasatch mountain range, looked down over the vast plain, and said, 'This is the place God wants us to be.'

Later other travellers arrived – some of them in search of silver. On the edge of the city you can still see grand houses built by those who were lucky enough to get rich on the mining.

Today, at this time of year, the travellers are mostly business people, and skiers. At the airport it's wise to keep a careful eye on travellers walking round with an unruly pair of skis on their shoulder.

Last year some 2.5 million people visited the Temple Square – the heartland of the Mormon faith. When you consider that the world-wide membership of the church is less than 6 million, that's a lot. People are *curious* about the Mormon faith. One reason is the missionary work that Mormons do – sending disciples in pairs to knock on people's doors. It can be hard work – two or three years in, say, West Germany, and gaining only twenty-two new baptised converts in all. But in America, the church's main problem, officials say, is how to cope with the rate of growth. There are new temples in Portland and Denver and other cities. And growth too, in the Far East – places like the Philippines and Japan, where the church's reverence towards ancestors is very attractive to eastern culture.

To the European mind, Mormonism seems a very American phenomenon indeed – a pioneer western religion that grew out of the Puritan idea of being a chosen people. It's a religion rooted in individualism and self-help. In his portraits, Joseph Smith, the church's founder, is a handsome man with blue eyes, sandy hair, and a prominent nose. In the 1820s and 1830s he had a series of revelations, through which, Mormons believe, God restored the original Christianity which had been lost to the earth. The Book of Mormon is a history of a group of people who came from Palestine about 600 BC, settled in the Americas and built a civilisation there. Their records were compiled by a prophet, on golden plates, and buried on a hill. Joseph Smith, it's claimed, received those plates from an angel, who commanded him to translate and publish them. They contained information of a visit of the resurrected Christ to these people. This new scripture is used by the Mormons alongside the Bible.

Although the landscape around Salt Lake City is oddly mystical – the strange salt lake, the hazy blueness, the wide deserts of the surrounding state of Utah – Mormonism is infused with a down-to-earth literalness which is strangely discordant. To Mormons, God has a flesh and blood body, exactly like that of a man except that it is immortal.

God is seen as the organiser rather than the creator of the universe. Organisation is certainly a Mormon strength. Like the Freemasons, Mormons have an impressive system of welfare for those who are sick or unemployed. And there's a clearly organised moral code, which forbids smoking, alcohol, tea or coffee, unfaithfulness and so on. In the early years, polygamy was practised. But this was officially dropped in 1890 since it contravened secular laws. Mormons take very seriously St Paul's words about respecting secular authority.

Mormons certainly take a lot of things very seriously – including the responsibility of trying to baptise all their ancestors who never had the opportunity to hear Mormon teachings.

In recent years a letter was published indicating that the church's founder Joseph Smith could have been involved in the occult. The man who sold this letter to the church is currently on a murder charge accused of causing the death of two church members by bomb attacks. The church now regards the letter as a forgery. Some church members have been severely disturbed by all this. But in Salt Lake City, there's every effort to carry on business as usual.

5 April 1986

Bible Belting

I see this week that more fire and brimstone is being flung around in the continuing fight between America's millionaire television evangelists. The defrocked pastor, Jim Bakker, and his wife are now saying they want to win back the 'Praise the Lord' (PTL) TV ministry from which they were sacked a couple of months back, after accusations of sexual immorality and financial greed. Meanwhile the country-and-western song writers are still cashing in. One lyric goes 'The PTL has gone to hell, so where do I send the money?'

But despite the huge setback all the scandal has caused the TV empires, many ministers in the local *main-line* churches are now allowing themselves a smile or two. For a *New York Times*/CBS poll has suggested that, despite all the hype that for years has surrounded the various TV ministries, viewers have been reckoning all along that they've been getting a better deal locally. Viewers were asked, 'Who has helped you more, ministers on TV or ministers at church?' Of those who just watched the programmes without sending money, only 5 per cent said 'TV', while 85 per cent said the local minister. And even among those who sent cheques, two-thirds said local ministers helped them more, compared with less than one in six who replied, 'TV preachers.' For as one commentator in the United States has put it, 'While the glamorous folks have basked in the limelight, these ministers have been on "bedpan" duty, in struggling little churches.'

One of the tensions between many such ministers and the evangelical-fundamentalist-pentacostal TV men has been the problem of how to approach the Bible.

Do you imply, for instance, that all of it – Old and New Testaments – is on a par as God's revealed word? Do you pick and choose bits of text, without discussing the context in which they were written? Do you dig out passages from the Old Testament and apply them indiscriminately to modern-day situations? This has been the sort of literal approach favoured by many TV evangelists, and it's caused deep concern among some other Christians, who say that the Bible just shouldn't be used like this.

This difference of approach is not new. In the nineteenth century some American feminists, for instance, launched a fierce attack on the Bible by interpreting it as literally as the most fundamental of fundamentalists. Take the book of Numbers, where Moses (apparently by God's orders) urges the Israelites to murder thousands of Midianites – male children and women. The feminists' argument was how could anyone possibly believe in a God like that?

But the answer of millions of Christians is of course that they *don't* believe in a God like that. They see the Bible as a record of *developing* faith, so that the more 'primitive' parts may be rejected in favour of the more 'advanced'. But how do believers decide what is more primitive and what is more advanced? The approach developed in most twentieth-century biblical scholarship is to test individual texts against the general thrust of the rest of the Bible. Murdering Midianite children doesn't fit too happily with loving your neighbour. Then the approach draws on reason, and it uses the combined experience of the prayer and action of believers through the centuries. These are the signposts for the journey towards God. Time and teaching are needed to make those signs clearer. Without them, the more simplistic of the TV evangelists will still have their day.

30 May 1987

8

SAINTS
AND SINNERS

Holy Island

If you take a strong pair of boots and go walking in the Northumberland hills, you can find a cave known as St Cuthbert's cave. From just up the wooded hill behind, there's a spectacular view of the long silvery coastline, and of Holy Island where Cuthbert was bishop 1,300 years ago. It was in glad memory of this man that over 1,000 people gathered last night in the floodlit splendour of Durham Cathedral to mark the anniversary of his death. So often Anglican services to mark centenaries can be formal, oddly impersonal events. But last night was not like that one bit. It was marvellously personal, a memory of a man to whom numerous churches in the north are still dedicated, a man who made the Christian life of holiness and prayer real in a world still in the grip of negative superstition and fear. Some of the place-names of that area are still based on Anglo-Saxon words for demons and goblins, reminders of another world where pagan religion still dominated.

What was it that was so special about that man that he's still remembered 1,300 years after his death?

We know more about him than most men of the time, thanks to the work of the first English historian, Bede, and an account from one of Cuthbert's brother monks. For many years Cuthbert was a hermit, living on a desolate barren island just off Holy Island, where the slate-coloured waters of the North Sea still crash against the rocks. But for a time he lived in the monastery at Holy Island itself. One night one of the monks followed him down towards the beach. Cuthbert went out into the sea until he was up to his arms and neck in the water. The splash of the waves accompanied his meditations through the dark hours of the night. At daybreak he came out, knelt on the sand and prayed. Then two otters bounded out of the water, stretched themselves out before him, warmed his feet with their breath and tried to dry him with their fur.

But Cuthbert was not just a hermit. He often did the rounds of the villages in the area, preaching the gospel, in places which were so remote and poor that others were daunted by the barbarity and squalor of the villagers' lives. There are many stories of how he healed people.

In a sermon last night the Archbishop of York said that saints do not belong in some never-never land. The world in which Cuthbert lived was divided by political and religious conflict.

At the time of his birth, Northumberland was attacked by invaders from Wales and the west. And the church was divided between those who supported the ancient Celtic traditions brought in from Ireland via Iona, and the Roman influences introduced from the continent. In himself he bridged the two traditions of the church, that of extreme Celtic asceticism and also the dignity and order of what it was to be a bishop in the Roman tradition. In the last months of his life, he returned to his barren island on Inner Farne to prepare himself for heaven.

Maybe the remarkable thing about Cuthbert was not just his closeness to the natural world, or his courage in difficult times, but that he lived out the meaning of his name, 'famous and bright'. In its history the light of the church has been kept shining through the lives of individual Christians, who have refused to get bogged down in disputes and quarrels, but who have lived lives of such holiness that their memories are still loved centuries later. Cuthbert has much to say to the church today.

14 March 1987

Mary Mother

I have to report a new angle on Christmas this year. Walt Disney characters. Their icons are now hanging above London's main shopping streets as part of the Christmas decorations. They reminded me of a recent court case in America about whether town councils should in fact spend *any* money *at all* on Christmas decorations. Some non-Christians didn't see why a proportion of their rates should be spent on marking other people's religious festivals. In the end the ruling was that town Christmas decorations were OK because they marked a cultural celebration rather than a religious event. In other words, you Christians can have the decorations, provided they don't mean anything. How's that for an insult?

If you talk to Christians about their beliefs, it's surprising how many are uncertain about one element of the Nativity stories – the doctrine of the Virgin Birth. One of those grappling with this yet again is the Bishop of Durham, David Jenkins. In his December diocesan letter, he says Christians have no right to insist on the literal truth of the virginity of Mary. Virgin Birth stories, he says, are not unique to the founder of Christianity and he goes on, 'There are serious critical and historical grounds for treating that story as one of the very early embroideries around the wonder of the discovery that this Jesus is God for us.' 'Many stories in the gospel', he adds, 'are "for real" not by being literally true, but by being inspired symbols of a living faith about the real activity of God. To insist on literal language as being the only way, or even the principal way, of bearing witness to God', he says, 'is to get stuck in something very close to magic and superstition.'

Perhaps I can here outline some of the theological discussion about the Virgin Birth. The gospels of St John and St Mark do not refer directly to the birth of Christ at all. But doubts about the historical accuracy of this story as told by Matthew and

Luke have been raised on several grounds. First, both Matthew and Luke give lists of Jesus' ancestors, traced back not through Mary, but through *Joseph*. If Joseph was not the father, then why are these lists given? Second, it's thought the story could have been told to fulfil a prophecy in Isaiah quoted in the New Testament about a young woman who will conceive and bear a son called Emmanuel. The New Testament Greek, it's argued, mistranslates as 'virgin' the Old Testament Hebrew word for 'young woman'. But another point made is that the infancy stories, as professions of faith, are intended in any case to make known not primarily historical truth, but *saving* truth. The story of the Virgin Birth is a way of expressing therefore that Mary was blessed in a unique way by God, and that her Son came from God and was filled with the Holy Spirit. It is a symbolic way of emphasising a profound and marvellous truth about the nature of Christ.

But many Christians would still see the Virgin Birth as historical truth as well as saving truth. And there are *reasons* for believing it happened, even though the event can never finally be proved one way or the other. For one thing, there were persistent hints in the gospels and elsewhere that there was something unusual about the birth of Jesus. The insults of a Jewish crowd implied he was illegitimate. In Mark another crowd referred to him as the son of Mary, whereas the normal practice was to describe a boy as the son of his father. And after all, Luke was a doctor, and regarded himself as a historian. Strange that a man so used to the facts of life and almost certainly someone who knew Mary personally, should have gone out of his way to include material which, if not intended to be historical, is at odds with the rest of his writing.

Of course, Bishop Jenkins doesn't demand that all Christians agree with him. But he does want his interpretation accepted as a valid way of understanding the Nativity.

But at Christmas, most people will not be talking too much about the whys and hows, but letting the power of those stories work on their imaginations.

1 December 1984

Savage Saints

This week a leading bishop has accused the authors of the gospels of St Matthew and St John and the book of Acts of anti-Semitism. The Bishop of Salisbury, Dr John Austin Baker, is one of four contributors to a church booklet called *Theology and Racism*. In an eighteen-page article, he says that Christianity must take a major share of the blame for Nazi genocide and that the church should now publicly admit its guilt, and disown what he describes as certain 'distorted features' of the New Testament.

The booklet is the latest contribution to a growing debate in theological circles about the relationship between Judaism and Christianity. It's a subject which, if explored in any depth at all, is enough to turn the stomach and bring a blush to the cheek of most modern Christians. The fact is that hatred of the Jews was taught and preached, as one Catholic scholar has put it, 'not simply by marginalised cranks, but by canonised saints, and that this state of affairs was tolerated and encouraged by the highest authorities in the church'. St Ambrose defended some people who had set a synagogue on fire on the grounds that it was a house of impiety. St Gregory of Nyssa condemned the Jews as 'a brood of vipers, slanderers, scoffers, an assembly of demons'. As for St John Chrysostom – a man described by the nineteenth-century English scholar Cardinal Newman as a 'bright gentle soul, a sensitive heart' – he described a synagogue as 'worse than a brothel. A temple of demons devoted to idolatrous cults.' The abuse expressed itself in legal restrictions. In the year 538, for instance, the synod of Orleans declared that Jews were not permitted to show themselves in the streets during Passion Week. In 1215, the Fourth Lateran Council decreed that Jews must be marked with a badge. In 1267 the synod of Breslau ordered compulsory Jewish ghettos.

In later years the writings of the reformer Martin Luther

again and again reflected anti-Jewish obsession. And, says Bishop Baker in his article, 'It's quite astonishing now to read the works of such a highly revered and loved Christian writer as G. K. Chesterton and to see how deeply, unthinkingly ingrained in him was a contemptuous, ignorant and misinformed anti-Semitism.'

The argument these days is not whether Christians have in the past been virulently anti-Jewish – the verdict must be guilty – but how far these attitudes have been based on a fair interpretation of the Bible texts or on a distorted understanding of them. If it is the former, then should these texts be disowned? And if so, on what basis?

At the root of Christian anti-Semitism is really the argument that the guilt of Christ's death should be placed not on the individual Jews who cried out to Pontius Pilate 'Crucify him', but on the whole race of Jews throughout future ages. The whole Jewish race is found guilty of deicide – the murder of God. Let me quote some of the biblical texts that have been used to support this view. Take for instance Matthew, chapter 27, verse 25, where after Pilate says 'I am innocent of the blood of this just person', according to the gospel writer the crowd shouted, 'His blood be on us, and on our children.' In John, chapter 19, the Jews are said to reply to Pilate, 'We have a law, and by our law he ought to die.' Bishop Baker believes that in the book of Acts the vast majority of Jews are presented as utterly bigoted and unscrupulous in their hostility to, and persecution of, the Christians. The effect of such texts, it's suggested, is to encourage Christians, while reading the accounts of the Passion, to see themselves and Jesus in opposition to the whole Jewish community.

But some modern biblical historians say this is factually inaccurate. They argue that, while legalism and corruption *were* to be found in first-century Israel, these distortions of Judaism were in fact being denounced by new movements within the community. Some scholars argue that when the writer of St John's gospel attacks the Jews, he's condemning not race or people, but opposition to Jesus. The word Jew, they

claim, symbolises any person, Christian or non-Christian, Jewish or pagan, who would reject with full knowledge the news of
salvation through Christ. After all, most of the writers of the
New Testament were Jews – though they felt themselves excluded from the Jewish community.

Bishop Baker asks Christians to remember that Jesus himself
was a Jew, that thousands of Jews formed the first Christian
churches, that the Jewish scriptures constituted for nearly 200
years the only Christian Bible. And he bases his call for the
church to disown what he calls 'distorted parts' of the Bible on
the Bible itself. The Bible as a whole, he says, commits us to a
deeper and larger view. And part of that view, he believes, is
that the *true* family of God is the *whole* of mankind.

2 March 1985

On the Feast of Stephen

Yesterday was not only Boxing Day, but the Feast
of St Stephen. That's the day, you remember, when Good
King Wenceslas looked out. In trudging through the snow to
take food, wine and fuel to 'yonder peasant' by St Agnes foun-
tain, Wenceslas was following in the footsteps of St Stephen
himself who was one of the seven deacons appointed by the
apostles to look after the distribution of gifts to the faithful, as
well as to help with preaching.

The name Boxing Day is associated with such giving. In the
old days, representatives of firms used to deliver Christmas
boxes to each other after Christmas, and apprentices would
visit their masters' clients collecting 'tips' in earthenware boxes
in recognition of their services through the year. But the most
likely explanation of the name Boxing Day was that this was the
day that the parson opened the church alms box, the poor box of
the parish, and distributed the contents to those in need. That's
why, incidentally, Parliament accepted in 1976 that if Christmas Day falls on a Saturday, Boxing Day is not the Sunday but

the following Monday. One MP explained to the House that in times past the parish priest was too busy to open the poor box on a Sunday.

Stephen's work as a deacon, looking after those who needed help, ended when he was stoned to death outside Jerusalem – the first martyr of the Christian church. One of the things he told the guard before his murder was that God does not live in houses made by men. Heaven is his throne and earth his footstool. These words warning against identifying God too much with particular holy places came home when I heard the story of the founding earlier this century of a children's clinic on the walls of the old city in Jerusalem near the Damascus Gate. It's a bit like a modern version of King Wenceslas.

It was Christmas Eve 1925 and a woman called Bertha Vester was the hostess of a very happy party, celebrating the start of the festival. As darkness fell the whole party decided to set out towards the shepherds' fields on the outskirts of the city. They left the house thrilled and excited at the prospect of singing carols in the fields, with the stars winking in the velvet, midnight-blue sky above and the lights of Bethlehem flickering in the far distance. As she was hurrying down the hill to catch up with the others, Mrs Vester met a woman trudging with great difficulty up the hill, helped along by a man. She was carrying a small bundle of dirty rags. Mrs Vester asked the man where they were going. 'Allah knows,' he said. *He* certainly did not know. He had spent the last six hours or so, travelling, trying to find a hospital which would take in his wife and their newly born child. But they had discovered that the hospitals were closed. The husband explained that he understood it was because there was a feast that day.

Mrs Vester was deeply touched. It seemed strange to her that here she was, rushing off to sing carols in the shepherds' fields to commemorate the birth of a babe who was born in a stable, and placed in a manger because there was no room at the inn. And here before her stood a woman with a child, and no room for them either at the inn. So Mrs Vester did not go to Bethlehem that night. Instead she did everything she could to find a hospital bed for the sick woman. She herself fed and bathed the child. On Christmas Day the mother died, and her husband came to the house saying that if he took the baby back to his cave home, the child would die. So Mrs Vester took in the baby and named him Noel, as a memory of that Christmas. A few days later more babies who needed homes joined the household, and more. That's how the Spafford clinic was born. I suspect Stephen would have approved.

27 December 1986

St Valentine

The Prime Minister's son, Mark Thatcher, gets married today. His bride is, as the popular papers put it, 'Texan beauty, deeply religious Diane Burgdorf, 26'. The wedding is to take place at London's Savoy Chapel, and they've chosen St Valentine's Day.

Who St Valentine was, is hard to discover. But tradition, that hardy plant, tells us he lived, and was martyred, in the third century, under the Roman Emperor Claudius II. Valentine apparently resisted un-Christian edicts by the emperor and for this he was beaten with clubs. Claudius had ruled that soldiers shouldn't marry, since domesticity, he reckoned, turned them soft. But Valentine performed marriages in secret. Eventually he was gaoled. And the romantic if unhistorical story goes that he fell in love with the gaoler's daughter, and she with him. On the day he was led out to be beheaded, he's supposed to have left a little note in the cell addressed to her and signed 'Your Valentine'.

In medieval England on Valentine's Day it was the custom for girls to tie coloured ribbons round their bedheads, and eat special foods to induce dreams of who was to be their husband. There was a tradition, too, that the first unmarried man a girl met on the day, would eventually marry her.

In the mid-seventeenth century the Puritans abolished all

this as too irreligious by half but following the Restoration in 1660, Valentine's Day continued as before. Take this entry in Samuel Pepys's diary, for instance:

February 14th [1661]. Up early, and to Sir [William] Batten's, but could not go in till I asked whether they that opened the door was a man or a woman, and [the manservant] answered 'A woman', which, with his tone, made me laugh: so up I went, and took Mrs Martha for my valentine, and Sir William he go in the same manner to my wife, and so we were very merry.

The tradition that the first man a woman met on Valentine's morning became her valentine was obviously continuing strong. For the following year, when Mrs Pepys had the painters in decorating the chimneypiece, she had to hold her hands over her eyes all morning so that she might not see the painters till after William Bowyer, her valentine, arrived.

Over the last few years the number of saints recognised by the church has shrunk through prunings and redundancies. St Wilgefortis, for instance, who was once invoked by maidens who wanted to get rid of unwanted suitors – rather handy if Valentine's Day got out of hand – never in fact existed.

It's widely known that St Cecilia was the traditional patron saint of musicians. But what about junk dealers (St Sebastian), rag and bone men (St Roch) and playing card manufacturers (St Balthasar)? Even truss-makers have their saint – it's St Lambert of Maastricht. The whole idea of patron saints depends on the understanding of the church as a family united in heaven and on earth. Lying behind it is the Christian teaching that communication within this family is not interrupted by death, but only changed. There is of course even a patron saint for us journalists. He's St Francis de Sales, who also happens to be patron saint to the deaf. No connection of course . . .

14 February 1987

Wycliffe the Unwelcome

Next Monday – the last day of the year – is the six-hundredth anniversary of the death of one of those troublesome priests who have helped to keep the light of faith burning through the centuries. He was John Wycliffe, an English theologian whose best claim to fame is as the driving force behind the first-ever English translation of the complete Bible. He grabbed the church by the scruff of its neck and forced it to have a good look at itself in the mirror. When part of the image it saw was one of greed and laziness and corruption, church leaders recoiled. When Wycliffe questioned the interpretation of certain doctrines, the Pope condemned his views as heretical, and his books were burnt as far away as Prague. Forty years after his death, his remains were dug up and burnt. The ashes were scattered on the River Swift, which flows past his church in Lutterworth, Leicestershire, in order that 'no trace be found of him again'.

Strange that so many of his ideas are now accepted in the world-wide church. And strange to muse on whether the great turmoils of the Reformation a century and a half later might have been avoided had the church heeded more seriously Wycliffe's red-light warnings earlier.

Wycliffe's century rather like our own had its share of problems. It was an unstable time. England was ruled by the senile and reclusive Edward III. Economic problems were aggravated by war with France. But the church had problems too. The Pope was at that time in exile in Avignon. England grudgingly acknowledged his authority, but challenged his control over many of the rich ecclesiastical appointments. A number of English benefices were occupied by Italians, Frenchmen and other foreigners. The Pope received five times more than the king in revenue. Pardons were sometimes hawked for money rather than for true repentance.

Wycliffe argued for sweeping changes in the church. He wanted people in monastic orders to be released from vows he regarded as unnatural and immoral. He attacked the system whereby a tenth of people's income was given to the church. If priests were not worthy, he said, they should not be given support. 'I demand', he said, 'that the poor inhabitants of our towns and villages be not constrained to furnish a worldly priest, often a vicious man and a heretic, with the means of satisfying his ostentation, his gluttony and his licentiousness, by buying a showy horse, costly saddles, bridles with dangling bells, rich garments and soft furs while they see the wives and children of their neighbours dying with hunger.'

To begin with, Wycliffe's condemnations of the corruptions in the church and the power and influence of the papacy received a ready ear among nationalist politicians. The parliament of the day supported the crown against the Pope. And John of Gaunt, the son of Edward III, helped to protect Wycliffe when the reformer was called to old St Paul's Cathedral to account for his views before the then Bishop of London. But in 1381 Wycliffe attacked the doctrine of transubstantiation. He declared that he did not believe that the words of the priest in the communion service changed the substance of the bread and wine into the actual body and blood of Christ. John of Gaunt hurried to Oxford to warn Wycliffe to keep silent on the matter, but he refused. In an appeal to Parliament, he argued that to persuade people that the sacrament was not bread but merely looks like it was contrary to the Scriptures. Indeed, he went on, you might just as well persuade people that a priest who was guilty of murder was really not such a man at all.

It was not long before Wycliffe was forced out of Oxford University. He spent his last two years at Lutterworth. There he completed his mission and got the Bible translated into English. One historian of the period complained that the effect of the translation had been to throw pearls before swine.

The part of the western church led from Rome still sometimes gives a good impression of being monolithic and unchanging. But over the last six centuries it has in fact undergone a slow process of evolution, and has taken on board some of Wycliffe's ideas which once seemed so heretical.

Today the system of paying for pardons has long been swept away, the Bible is easily available, priests are expected to look after the people in their areas, even *services* are in the everyday language of the people. As for the vast papal lands in Italy, for instance, these have been reduced to the Vatican City. Yet Wycliffe, I suspect, could today still be critical of the Vatican's finances and some of its doctrines. He would oppose the remaining ties between state and church in England. And he would try to revive the vigour of the nonconformist preaching ministry throughout Britain. Though he disliked the church of his day, he loved the Bible. He would find it a sad sight to see it on so many shelves, unread.

29 December 1984

Dictionary Johnson

Two hundred years ago next week died a man who towers above those of us today who still earn a living by journalism. I mean Dr Samuel Johnson, 'Dictionary Johnson', editor of Shakespeare, parliamentary reporter, and author of countless articles, poems, letters and journals.

I've just been re-reading John Wain's fine biography of him. It evoked again the stories of Johnson scribbling away half blind in his garret, hunched up over his desk, selecting and defining the words for the dictionary. And Johnson the great conversationalist, ensconced in a seat by the tavern fire, calling out in his Midlands accent, 'Who's for Poonsh?', and sparring with the painter Reynolds or Garrick the actor.

I love his work for its humanity. Take his biography of the poet, Richard Savage – he portrays Savage's brilliant and charming personality, but also builds up an inexorable portrait of how those who tried to help him were often discouraged, and then torn by his outrageous behaviour. For with Johnson, you feel he is trying to tell you the truth. In those days journalists were not allowed to report the proceedings of Parliament. So Johnson was commissioned by the *Gentleman's Magazine* to make up the speeches of the various powerful lords and honourable members, in a series of so-called parliamentary debates. But when Johnson discovered that people were believing these reports to be true, he was appalled, and immediately stopped writing them. Even in small matters he was scrupulous. He would never allow his manservant to say he was out if he was in and merely didn't want to see anyone.

He had bouts of useless dejection, which he regarded with guilt and shame. He spoke of the mercy of God, but he felt, with a terrible seriousness, the feared damnation. When asked by a sweetly reasonable clergyman what he *meant* by damnation, Johnson roared out, 'Sent to hell, sir, and punished everlastingly!'

In 1767, at about ten o'clock one Saturday morning, he took his earthly leave of Catherine Chambers, a dying woman who had for years been his mother's companion. Most of us today would join other friends in the room, try to say a few quiet and loving things, perhaps sit in silence for a while. Johnson asked everyone to withdraw, told her quietly but frankly they were to part for ever, and then asked if she was willing for him to say a short prayer beside her, since as Christians they should part in prayer. She apparently held up her poor hands with great fervour as she lay in bed, while he prayed kneeling beside her. He prayed first of all that God would visit and relieve her. Next that God would grant that her sense of weakness would add strength to her faith, and seriousness to her repentance. And last that they all might obtain everlasting happiness through Jesus Christ. Then they kissed and parted with tenderness.

To say he was a moralist sounds these days like a slur. But he *was* a moralist, and a great one. He knew in his early days in London what it was like to be poor, and to have nowhere to lay your head at night, and to be desperate for work, and then to be employed for a sum that mocked the energy and effort spent.

In a sense it strengthened his conviction in classical values; he believed in a hierarchical society, stable and solid, where those with fortune and favour behaved generously and humanely to those less fortunate. A high Anglican himself, he disliked Methodists, Quakers, Presbyterians and nonconformists of all sorts as a threat to the stability of the religious and social order.

Johnson's own household in later years, after the death of his wife, was bizarre. He generously shared his home with a motley collection mostly of old age pensioners, who had little in common, it seems, except that they were poor and quarrelsome. Apart from Frank Barber, a young mulatto and something of a ladies' man, there was a blind Miss Williams, a morose physician, a widow and a woman whom Johnson once described as a stupid slut! They got by on a fixed allowance he gave them all.

For Johnson, though he was sometimes eccentric, sometimes contradictory, tried to live in the light of the values he held sacred. A moralist yes, but never a hypocrite.

8 December 1984

9

RIGHT
AND WRONG

Fighting Talk

Last weekend [2–3 April] we all heard so much about the various anti-nuclear demos and the factions on all sides claiming to stand for peace, that I started to have a good think about why, when we all want peace, we still so often opt for aggression. I was encouraged by a lecture I heard on Wednesday at St James's Church, Piccadilly, London, entitled 'The Inevitability of Conflict'. There was no question mark after the title and, as one member of the audience pointed out, the speaker needed to be congratulated on the choice of the title. For after all, no one could dispute the statement that conflict was inevitable without conflicting with the speaker!

The lecturer was Dr Anthony Stevens, 'a psychotherapist, psychologist and psychiatrist'. I'll leave you to sort out the distinctions between those labels. But the gist of what he had to say was that he was worried about the tendency of some people to talk of peace as if it could be achieved by rational thought. The dangerous tendency, he said, was to consider conflict a rational phenomenon, with rational explanations. In other words, he was deeply sceptical of the notion that conflict could be eliminated only by improvements in housing, education, sharing of wealth, etc., etc.

The origins of conflict, he said, were not rational, but biological. And until this was properly recognised by us all, talk about peace was unrealistic, naïve and potentially dangerous.

Well, he went on to illustrate his point by referring to scientific studies. Neurological studies have shown there are rage centres within animals and these have been demonstrated in humans too. By passing electrical currents through a certain point in the human brain, people can be stimulated to feel wildly furious. Moreover aggressiveness can be stimulated by increases in male hormones. The effect of this rage centre, he argued, is that conflict is inevitable both within all societies – at all levels – and within ourselves. It is tied in with a human compulsion to polarise and to take sides. Also to win and defend territory and resources.

Dr Stevens went on to say that when a society has been at peace with its neighbours for a period, then conflict within the society itself intensifies. That could certainly help to explain why, for instance, the crime rate here was so much lower directly after the war, and could be one reason why it has risen since.

At this point I looked round the audience and saw they were beginning to feel as depressed as I was about this apparently fatalistic message. But Dr Stevens denied that it was fatalistic. He maintained that one way of keeping some sort of peaceful balance was by equilibrium – a balance of forces. This clearly has implications for the nuclear argument.

Disappointingly, he had little to say about the place of *Christian* ideas in all this. He certainly sees the Christian injunction to love our enemies as an attempt to override the biological human urge towards conflict. He did agree with one questioner that one priority was to work out methods of channelling conflict creatively.

But his paper left many questions unanswered, though it did point to an area, it seemed to me, that had to be taken seriously. It underlined perhaps the obvious fact that no one can force other people into peaceful attitudes if they are in fact driven by an irrational desire for conflict. And that if Christians and other people who take religious experience seriously are to be taken seriously themselves, then peace must begin in their own hearts. And I suppose that means taking *prayer* seriously. The Buddhists have a meditation exercise, where they concentrate first on someone they love. They then move on to a less close friend, then to an acquaintance, and finally to someone with whom they are in conflict. The aim of the meditation is to maintain a state of inner spiritual peace, which can absorb conflict. A theologian I much admire once said that his experience of prayer had been that in praying seriously for his enemies, he had come to the point where his own feelings of aggression had evaporated.

I put this point once to Enoch Powell. Yes, he said, you can love your enemies, but you still have to go out and shoot them, don't you?

9 April 1983

War and Peace

If you're passing any bookshops today, you might come across a slim black paperback ambitiously titled *The Challenge of Peace: God's Promise and Our Response*. It's the full text of the historic pastoral letter of the United States Roman Catholic bishops denouncing nuclear war. This was the letter that took them three drafts, 500 amendments, and two years and a few white hairs, to write. It was finally agreed by the bishops in Chicago in May this year by the overwhelming vote of 238 to nine. As they filed out of the meeting hall, they were warmly applauded by a group of peace demonstrators. It was a time, wrote one reporter, for reflection and quiet exultation.

And reading the letter's ninety-four pages again this week, I'm not surprised that it's created such a stir in the United States. Let me give you a flavour of the contents.

In the letter, the bishops utterly condemn the indiscriminate taking of many innocent lives by nuclear weapons. Moreover, they rule out the *first* use of nuclear weapons in *any* circumstances. They express extreme scepticism about the possibility of waging a limited nuclear war that would meet the standards of the churches' traditional 'just war' theory of justifiable self-defence. They endorse the concept of a nuclear freeze.

As for the basic principle of nuclear deterrence itself, that they find acceptable only if the United States is pursuing serious talks on arms reductions. The bishops pledged themselves to go without meat on Fridays and to do penance and to pray. And they ask other Roman Catholics to follow their example as a means of expressing their concern about peace.

Well, you may ask, is all this so very radical? After all, we've got used these days to some Christians condemning nuclear deterrence altogether. The *Scottish* Roman Catholic bishops, for instance, have declared it immoral not only to *use* nuclear weapons, but even to *threaten* to use them. Is it really logical for the American bishops to allow deterrence (however hedged about with conditions) if at the same time they imply that they can hardly conceive of any circumstances which would justify the use of a nuclear weapon? Surely a deterrent only works if the other side thinks you might use it?

So why has the letter caused such a flurry? One reason is that the American bishops do after all belong to the nation that was the first to produce atomic weapons. The United States has been the only nation to use them, and today is one of the handful of nations capable of decisively influencing the course of the nuclear age. The second reason is that over a quarter of the members of the American armed services are Roman Catholics. What would happen if they refused to obey orders to fire a nuclear weapon?

But another factor is that the letter was so clearly written with such painstaking care. Typical of the bishops' care is their opening analysis of what the word 'peace' means anyway. Not for them the merely secular concept of peace as the absence of war. Their vision of peace emerges from the biblical version of peace with justice, a right relationship with God, and the hope of the final full realisation of God's salvation.

The letter marks two milestones. First it represents the extraordinary change that has taken place in the Roman Catholic Church in the USA in recent years. Thirty years ago, it's hardly conceivable that the Roman Catholic bishops would have issued a letter placing them in opposition to important aspects of government policy. The Roman Catholic Church in the States was then largely composed of immigrants. One effect of that was a tendency to super-patriotism in compensation for any suspicions that they were not loyal citizens. The second milestone is that the letter has established a precedent for open public debate among the bishops on key moral issues. In the past the style of the Roman Catholic bishops around the world has usually been to meet behind closed doors, and in cases of disagreement to say nothing or to issue pious, but vague statements. But the American bishops were brave enough to debate the issue in public and to allow the press to hear their long discussions with generals and defence experts, theologians and the rest. The effect was to stimulate moral debate in parishes around the United States. It's a lesson that the Roman Catholic bishops in this country might do well to consider.

27 August 1983

Marriage à la Mode

If, in an idle moment, you browse through a list of the cardinals and archbishops of the international Roman Catholic Church, the names can provide some mildly diverting reading. The name Cardinal Sin of the Philippines is too well known these days to raise a smile, but there's a Cardinal Wako (memories of Jimmy Edwards) and some years ago the Vatican appointed as prefect of the Vatican Library and papal archivist, an Archbishop Stickler. No books too long overdue there, I expect.

But one beautiful name is that of Cardinal Otunga from Kenya, who is, I believe, somewhat exceptional in the college of cardinals for having getting on for a hundred brothers and sisters. His father was a pagan tribal chieftain, with over a dozen wives. His father was converted and Cardinal Otunga himself was baptised at the age of twelve.

Becoming a Christian in such circumstances has all sorts of cultural implications – and not least the question of how to adapt to the Christian understanding of marriage being a union between one man and one woman. No doubt this was one of the things the cardinal's father pondered as he learnt about Christianity. But he was converted and changed the habits of his adult life by living from then onwards with only one of his many wives. This follows the guidelines concerning such converts laid down by Rome. It's an interesting illustration of how radical in a society like that, the Christian understanding of marriage is.

Jesus' teaching about marriage being the lifelong union of one man with one woman, and his prohibiting of divorce, must have been heard in first-century Palestine with a similar sense of shock.

I was reminded of that this week when reading a paper on marriage prepared some years ago for the United Reformed Church by Andrew Hodgson. It points out that in the history of how various societies have tried to regulate sexual relations, two general characteristics are common. First that men have almost invariably regarded women as available to them for their use, rather like chattels. For instance, he points out that the tenth commandment forbids men coveting their neighbour's house (that is, property), wife, stock and servants. It's striking that the prohibition is addressed to men and that 'wife' appears second in the list after 'property'. Secondly, says Mr Hodgson, it's been almost universally accepted that male sexual desire is not satisfied with one wife. A wide range of customs can be found recognising extramarital relations, with concubines or prostitutes. Tradition had it that King David had 400 wives and his son more. The patriarch Abraham himself took a second wife to bear him a child and it seems that no general movement towards one man one wife can be traced until the period of Greek influence, in the centuries before Christ. Even towards the later period of Roman domination, the teaching of the rabbis merely discouraged polygamy; rather than forbidding it. So Jesus was talking to a society where even if monogamy may by then have been considered the norm, successive marriage was very common. Certainly men could divorce women easily, and any real equality between men and women within marriage was practically inconceivable. Into this Jesus stepped, and dared to teach an equality of men and women in his prohibition of divorce.

If Jesus was concerned about equality, and real responsibility in marriage, that raises the interesting question of what responsibility a man has to his several wives once he has become a Christian. Would it be more 'Christian' in a sense to keep those wives, provided of course that he marries no more? After all from the woman's point of view it could be an appalling shock to be 'cast off'.

Well, this sort of discussion has been going on in the church for many years. The Anglican church in Kenya has now adopted a regulation by which a man with several wives who is then baptised and confirmed may take communion without putting away any of his wives. When this was discussed at the international meeting in Nigeria last year of representatives from Anglican churches around the world, the feeling was that the Kenyan church had chosen the lesser of two wrongs. The greater wrong would have been to dismiss the man's dependent wives, or to refuse him communion. The lesser wrong was to make careful exception to normal church regulations by accepting the situation, provided of course that he took no more wives. Some Kenyan Anglicans found this grudging approval somewhat puzzling. They pointed out that a number of Anglican churches around the world are now marrying some divorcees during the lifetime of a previous partner. The Church of England is currently agonising over the issue. And with so many cultural, ethical and historical factors involved, it's perhaps not surprising that a consensus is hard to achieve. But to the Kenyans, remarrying divorcees looks remarkably like approving polygamy – even if it is only one spouse at a time.

9 February 1985

Irish Ayes and Irish Noes

Every few years the people of the Republic of Ireland turn away with something approaching relief from worries about the economic and other problems that plague their country. Instead – almost cheerfully – they return to a heart-searching anguished debate about subjects like contraception, divorce and abortion. At present Ireland is the only European country that bans divorce. For weeks now the radio and television and press have been full of arguments about whether or not the constitution of the republic should be changed to allow divorce. Early opinion polls in April indicated a majority of 22 per cent backing the government's desire to bring the legislation of the country in line with that of modern, liberal, secular democracies. But in the end, on Thursday [26 June] in a national referendum, the country's voters decisively voted against any change.

The Roman Catholic bishops stopped short of telling Catholics outright to vote no in the referendum. But their influence was no doubt the most powerful factor in the vote. The bishops, collectively and individually, have argued on two levels: scriptural references, and estimates of the likely consequences of allowing divorce.

In a joint statement published earlier this month, the bishops quoted Matthew, chapter 19. 'What God has united, man must not divide.' They then went on to speak of the Christian ideal of lifelong marriage. But there was no discussion of the conflicting biblical evidence on marriage. For instance, although absolute prohibition of divorce is indicated twice in the gospels, an exception for adultery is made in Matthew. The position of many Protestants is that the Bible is not very clear whether Christ was describing an ideal or laying down a law for all subsequent civil law on the matter. It's clear, however, that he was repudiating the ease with which, in the first century,

Israel's men could discard their wives.

But the bishops' arguments went on to concentrate strongly on the effects of divorce. It would, they said, increase the number of broken marriages. This week Cardinal O'Fiaiach, the leader of the Roman Catholic Church in Ireland, gave some Northern Ireland figures to support his case. He said divorce there had now reached the proportions of an epidemic. Since the introduction in 1979 of 'no fault' divorce in the north, divorce rates had jumped from one in forty marriages in 1970 to one in five last year. As a result the divorce rate was nearly half as high as England, which is one of the highest in the world.

Other anti-divorce groups painted a sad picture of the future fate of Ireland if it followed such a path. Their opponents have accused some of them of using inaccurate statistics and half-truths.

One response made to the cardinal's argument is that Catholic society in Ireland is so very different from the secular, post-Christian society of England and the United States, that divorce even if allowed is unlikely to be very widespread. In Italy, for instance, the divorce rate is only one-fourteenth that of England. One reason for that is the very strong sense of family in a country where government has tended to be weak, jobs hard to find and social services thin.

Much of this debate has assumed that allowing divorce in the republic would contradict, or at least sit uneasily with, the teachings of the Roman Catholic Church. But one area which the bishops seem to have avoided – publicly at least – is whether their declared position in effect contradicts the declaration on religious freedom made by the Second Vatican Council. 'The human person', the council said, 'has a right to religious freedom . . . In matters religious, no one is to be restrained from acting in accordance with his own beliefs within due limits.' Indeed in 1984 the Bishop of Down and Connor, Dr Cahal Daly, made this declaration to the New Ireland Forum. 'We bishops', he said, 'would raise our voices to resist any constitutional proposals which might endanger the civil or religious

rights and liberties cherished by Northern Ireland Protestants.'
But since divorce is not allowed in Ireland, such people who
wish to act in accordance with their belief are prevented from
doing so by the state. So should the church therefore demand
that the constitution should be changed?

The referendum seems like a victory for Catholic teaching.
But a number of Catholics believe it is not.

28 June 1986

Worrying about Warnock

The other day I heard a joke about the current
arguments in the House of Commons over the morality of the
Warnock Committee's recommendation that licensed research
should be allowed on human embryos for the first fourteen days
of life. The joke centred on the question of the status of the
embryo, and the respect consequently due to it. It had a woman
sitting up in a hospital bed saying crossly to a male doctor, 'I
demand respect – after all I was once a potential human being.'

This story made me laugh out loud, because I heard it
directly after sitting through a particularly obtuse debate on the
subject of Warnock at the Church of Scotland's General Assembly a fortnight ago. It ended with the assembly opposing
any experimentation on embryos. That means the assembly
now shares the views of the Roman Catholic bishops. In February the Church of England's synod by a narrow majority came
to a similar conclusion.

Briefing papers have served mostly, it seems, to make many
Christians so confused by the complexities that they have
tended to grasp at the simplest response – a clear 'no' to research. That's not to say that such gut feelings are necessarily
wrong. But they do not seem to be based on very much
information.

In the Church of Scotland debate, most people were uneasily
aware of the limitations of their knowledge. But the effect of

that was not, as you might think, caution, but a willingness to be swayed by anyone who sounded as if they knew about the subject. The assembly was strongly influenced by two particular arguments in a speech by the theologian Professor Tom Torrance, delivered in somewhat magisterial style. First he quoted the words of Jesus, 'Inasmuch as ye have done it unto one of the least of these my brethren, ye have done it unto me.' By a remarkable jump of logic, he managed to imply that Jesus was talking there about experiments on embryos. However, Professor Torrance provided no clear theological arguments backing up his belief that a newly fertilised egg is a human person. A second point was his declaration that to cross-fertilise was in his words 'indescribably horrendous'. Most members also felt a shiver of horror at the thought. And they voted against research.

What wasn't discussed in any detail was the distinction between different *types* of research. For Warnock did not recommend *unlimited* research for a period of fourteen days. It recommended *licensed* research. Now that licence could, for instance, specifically forbid cloning. It could also forbid genetic modification of embryos or their transfer to an animal's womb. It could demand a signed consent from parents of the embryo for its use in research. And the licensing authority could insist that any application to use embryos must give reasons why information cannot be obtained from studies of species other than human. All these suggestions have been made this week by a voluntary authority researching guidelines for licensing embryo research.

Of course all those Christians and others who believe that from the moment the egg is fertilised, the embryo is an unborn child, will not be interested in what they will see as such compromises. Cardinal Hume in an article this week added another reason why he opposed any research on embryos. He was really saying that the Warnock argument is a very slippery slope, because if you accept fourteen days as the outside limit for research, what's to stop you later changing it to twenty-one and twenty-eight and thirty, once research gets more interesting? We must not, he suggested, abandon objective moral principles. This argument appeals to many others who fear that any price will be paid for scientific advancement.

One of the church's great problems in ethical areas is that in the past it has sometimes claimed as moral absolutes positions which it later abandoned. At one time, for example, it refused to allow experiments on dead bodies. In 1745, the Roman Catholic Church outlawed interest on loans. It has, in fact, never officially rescinded this, even though it clearly no longer holds that view. Just because the church has shifted its views on some things, is not to say there *are* no moral absolutes.

But it *is* to say that what has historically been perceived as absolute, has not always in fact been so. That is one reason why scientist-theologians like the Archbishop of York are trying to warn that in complex areas like this one, moral absolution is not necessarily a mark of Christian integrity. But Cardinal Hume, among others, believes that in this particular case, the evidence has been weighed and the verdict is clear.

8 June 1985

10

IN GOOD
FAITH

Prison Walls

I doubt whether the news of President Andropov's death will have yet filtered through to all Soviet citizens. I was thinking of people like Alexander Ogorodnikov, Gleb Yakunin, Zoya Krakhmalnikova, Vladimir Poresh. The reason they may not have heard the news is that they are cut off from the rest of Soviet society. They're prisoners, serving a varying number of years in gaol, for violations of state laws. Common criminals you may say. Well, to Soviet officials and no doubt to Mr Andropov, yes. But to others, they are people who thought that religious freedom meant being free not only to worship in registered Soviet churches but to do things like distributing religious literature or organising religious study groups, communities and committees without official approval. There are over 300 known Christian prisoners of conscience in the USSR, and every now and again a letter or testimony from them is received in the west.

To give you some idea of the flavour of these letters, let me quote from someone called Anatoli Levitin:

The greatest miracle of all is prayer. I have only to turn my thoughts to God and I suddenly feel a force bursting into me; there is new strength in my soul, in my entire being . . . The basis of my whole spiritual life is the Orthodox liturgy, so while I was in prison I attended it every day in my imagination. At 8.00 in the morning I would begin walking round my cell, repeating its words to myself. I was then inseparably linked to the whole Christian world. In the Great Litany I would always pray for the Pope and for the Ecumenical Patriarch, as well as for the leaders of my own church. Then I would begin praying in my own words, remembering all those near to me, those in prison and those who were free, those still alive and those who had died. More and more names welled up from my memory . . . The prison walls moved apart and the whole universe became my residence, visible and invisible, the universe for which Christ's wounded, pierced body offered itself as a sacrifice . . . After this, I experienced an exaltation of spirit *all day* – I felt purified within. Not only my own prayer helped me, but even more the prayer of many other faithful Christians. I felt it continually, working from a distance, lifting me up as though on wings, giving me living water and the bread of life, peace of soul, rest and love.

Mr Levitin's letter reminded me of the words of a Lebanese Christian I know, suffering in a different place in different circumstances as the country and nation she loves is destroyed bit by bit, by shell and machine-gun fire and division and hatred. Whereas the British civilians may leave, for her there is no passage home.

This week the Pope has sent a seventy-page letter to her, and to all who, from whatever country, suffer or are depressed by the sufferings in today's world. It is a letter he has long been writing and it has grown especially out of his months' convalescing from the attempt on his life.

The key question he faces is how Christians are to understand the presence of such suffering in the world and especially innocent suffering. And the heart of the letter is his reflection on the meaning of Christ's suffering on the cross. Through that suffering he says Christ carries the greatest possible answer to the question why, because in the truth of his suffering, Christ *proved* the truth of his *love*. Through such suffering he absorbed and so annihilated the evil which caused it. It is in this sense that Christ takes upon himself the sins of all.

But how can this help those whose children have been killed in Beirut or elsewhere? Or who are trapped unable to see the sky in some rigorous Soviet gaol? It is through suffering, the Pope says, that those surrounded by the mystery of Christ's redeeming suffering become mature enough to enter his kingdom. Through suffering, men and women can reveal their potential moral greatness, their spiritual maturity.

It is a challenging vision, and one that I can hardly begin to suggest in this brief talk.

But the strength of the letter comes because it has been written not by a man who's spent his life in ecclesiastical libraries and is now theorising about the world, but a man some of whose friends died in Auschwitz, a man who has dedicated his life to the search for the answers to men's and women's most fundamental questions, and a man whose own life and health and confidence have been so threatened. In one sense this is part of the Pope's answer to his would-be Turkish assassin, Ali Agja.

11 February 1984

Who Reigns?

On Thursday evening about 3,000 people filled the glittering gold spaces of St Paul's Cathedral for a memorial service. It was for a man whose life and death challenged and encouraged the faith of hundreds of thousands of Christians throughout the United Kingdom. He was Canon David Watson, who died of liver cancer at his London home very early on Saturday 18 February 1984 at the age of fifty.

The congregation included the Archbishop of Canterbury, several bishops, and the leaders of the renewal movement in Britain. Among the Bible passages read were these lines from Psalm 91

Whoever goes to the Lord for safety,
Whoever remains under the protection of the Almighty
Can say to Him, 'You are my defender and protector.
You are my God. In you I trust.'

If there was one striking quality about David Watson, it was
that he trusted. He trusted in the Holy Spirit, he trusted that
God responded to faith – not always in ways that we understand
– and he trusted the biblical promise that nothing in all creation
could separate him from the love of God in Christ Jesus. On
this rock faith, his work flourished. When, some years ago, he
became rector of St Michael-le-Belfrey in York, the congregation was six. A few years later it was a living Christian community of 700. He experimented at some personal cost with
sharing a home and his income with other Christians. And he
developed a shared ministry with a team of preachers and
singers, actors and dancers to preach the gospel around the
country.

In some ways, as one of his friends pointed out in the memorial sermon, he seemed unsuited for the work of an evangelist.
For a start he had asthma, he occasionally had patches of dark
depression, and he regarded himself as a man who had devoted
so much energy to his work that he had sometimes failed as a
husband. But he genuinely and profoundly believed that God
could use any of us for his work, and was convinced that God
had not given up on the church. In one of his books, he
described an experience he had of being filled with the Holy
Spirit. One day, he wrote, he confessed every thing he could
think of, told the Lord he was willing to obey him whatever the
cost and then asked that he might be filled with the Spirit. As he
went on, he had a quiet and overwhelming sense of being
embraced by the love of God. It seemed the presence of God
filled the room.

I heard him preach on several occasions. During the last
months of his life, I interviewed him twice. He said that,
despite the cancer, he was convinced, though he could be
wrong, that he would be healed by God. He had, after all, seen

many other people healed during his ministry. He believed that such healing demanded not just the odd prayer, but that the person should be surrounded by the healing prayer and love of a Christian community.

Since he died, there has been a spate of articles in the Christian press about why he was not healed. Some people have said he died because those praying for him did not have enough faith. Others ask why in any case should *he* have been healed when the need of many others is so great? But the experience of many many Christians, now and throughout 2,000 years, is that prayer does sometimes release healing. This does not mean, as one priest has put it, that prayer is instructing God in his duties or ordering from him what is wanted. It is co-operating with him in fulfilling his purposes. He reigns – his people serve.

The night before his death, Jesus made his way as usual to the Mount of Olives, accompanied by his disciples. He withdrew himself from them about a stone's throw, knelt down and began to pray. 'Father, if it be thy will,' he said, 'take this cup away from me. Yet not my will but thine be done.' It was in imitation of that spirit that David Watson took the natural step of dying.

At his meetings he would often ask the congregation at the end to declare together confidently, 'The Lord reigns.' One of his friends asked the congregation at St Paul's to say those words. They hesitated as they said, 'The Lord reigns.' Over a needy world desperately needing Christ's love and a church that needs to be renewed, 'The Lord reigns', they said together more confidently. What about over the ravages of cancer and the ravages of death? There was a slight pause. Then, with a strong united voice, they declared together once more, 'The Lord reigns.'

7 April 1984

Corpus Christi

After the consecration yesterday of Professor David Jenkins as Bishop of Durham, the professor and the Archbishop of York came out on to the grass in the sunshine. As the cameramen surged forward, a sole protester shouted out, 'Heretic.' He was waving a placard, which said in effect that the Christian faith didn't exist unless Christians believed in the bodily resurrection of Christ.

One of the things that has struck me on several occasions over this controversy is the use of the word 'truth'. The protesters believe they have been defending truth, yet time after time, I have heard them accuse Professor Jenkins of saying things he has not said. It's been the technique of setting up Aunt Sallies and then knocking them down to your own satisfaction. I don't wish to suggest that this has been done maliciously. I think it has happened because people are genuinely confused about what Professor Jenkins *is* saying. And Professor Jenkins *can* be confusing in the way he expresses himself. But I've never heard him deny categorically the bodily resurrection of Jesus. When I put this yesterday to one of the men who disrupted the consecration, he hummed and ha'd and said that he'd read about it all in the papers and seen him on television and Professor Jenkins hadn't come clean on this doctrine. Yet a minute before he had told me categorically that Professor Jenkins didn't believe in the resurrection as a historical fact.

The point is of course what does *anyone* mean by the resurrection? Some of the protesters believe that at its root must be the physical raising of the body of Jesus. And they have some good arguments. For instance, when Thomas doubted, the risen Christ appeared and showed him the four nail holes on his crucified hands and feet. Thomas was invited to put his finger in these marks of Christ's torture. That all sounds physical enough, and the gospel goes to great lengths to catalogue the physical features of the story. But Christ also appeared to his disciples when they were in a locked room. If his risen body was as our bodies, then he couldn't have entered the room. The point is that the image of the physical body is in a sense only part of the description of what happened.

What Professor Jenkins is saying, is that because of problems like this we can't be sure *exactly* what physically happened. Christ's flesh and blood may have risen, they may not. It's impossible to tell 2,000 years later exactly what were the provable facts. In one sense the details don't matter to him very much. What does matter is the conviction that whatever did happen was enough to spark off a whole series of experiences in the hearts and minds of the early Christians that Christ's power and life and purpose and personality were a risen and living presence. This is his understanding of the resurrection.

You may ask why in that case are the creeds so specific about the Resurrection of the Body?

Well, in the sermon at York Minster yesterday, Professor Denis Nineham, another theologian, tried to explore the historical circumstances surrounding the creeds. He believes that the faith of the very early Christians would not have been expressed in those terms.

He argued that the creeds reflect the language and interests of Greek philosophy. He also pointed out that at the early church council where these things were discussed, terrible rows went on. The letters page of *The Times* looks mild, he says, compared with the violent abuse in some of the councils. One patriarch of Constantinople in the fifth century never recovered from the mugging given him by a group of monks at one council. In other words, there's always been discussion about these matters. He believes that it is only now with the challenge of the modern world that many things are being expressed differently.

The Archbishop of York said after the service that he hoped Christians would be able to discuss differences charitably. Certainly a lot of teaching and listening now needs to be done in the church. And it's not good enough for the more intellectual of the clergy to blame this present confusion on other people's lack of sophistication. They have to show that what they are saying does have an evangelistic message that really will illuminate the twentieth-century world. Otherwise the controversy will degenerate further into internal church bickering, and the vision of the world Christ wanted will get even more obscured.

7 July 1984

Sorry Sacrifice

Tomorrow is Remembrance Sunday so let me tell you a remembrance story. It's about a family of people called Kramer who during the Nazi occupation of Poland lived on the outskirts of a town called Vilna. At that time, the Nazis were shooting Jews on sight, and so Mr and Mrs Kramer and their baby son David, together with forty-three other Jews, went into hiding in a bunker. As the Nazis, searching the area, came closer to the bunker, the baby began to cry. Everyone was terrified the baby would give them away. Mr Kramer, the father of the child, hesitated for a long anguished moment; then he suffocated his own son. Today you can still find in an Israeli synagogue in Bat Yam a Torah scroll in memory of David. His sacrifice meant that all the others in the bunker managed to escape.

All of us would, I think, understand sacrifice in that sense. And tomorrow, people all over the country will be remembering other sacrifices, as the long roll-call of names is read out. To many of us, the names will not be known personally – we won't be able to remember the personalities and idiosyncrasies of those mentioned. But the names themselves tell their own story. In some villages up to ten will carry the same surname.

Today, individuals are still making sacrifices – whether it's struggling to look after someone who's ill, or to share an all too meagre income with other people. In some places the sacrifice might be given grudgingly and counted. But in others it's given freely and lovingly and generously. It's in this spirit of free and loving offering that Christians believe that Jesus sacrificed himself.

So why is it then that so many people find the Christian theology of sacrifice disturbing, even repellent? To be quite honest, for many years I found it so myself.

The problem *I* had was centred mostly on Victorian-style hymns which had verses like this:

O sinner, mark and ponder well
Sin's awful condemnation.
Think what a sacrifice it cost
To purchase thy salvation.

The impression such hymns can give was summarised in a letter I received lately. The writer recognised God as the sustainer and origin of the whole boundless universe. But, he said, people like him who would otherwise be attracted to religion are repulsed by the idea that God is petty: so peeved by childish humanity that he needs to be propitiated by a sacrifice – even to demand the death of his only Son. The word 'propitiate' means to placate an offended person. It is that sense that is used in the 1662 Anglican communion service, for instance, when it quotes the first Epistle of St John: 'If any man sin', it says, 'we have an advocate with the Father, Jesus Christ the Righteous, and He is the propitiation for our sins.'

Well, what does all this mean? Does it mean that the Christian teaching about sacrifice regards Jesus, the Lamb of God, in the same way as the animals sacrificed in the temple in Jerusalem in the first century? Thousands were offered to appease God's anger. I don't think it means that, though I think Christian teaching has become in some cases overlaid with the notion. Let me explain.

First of all, sacrifice was such an important part in the rituals of ancient (though not modern) Judaism, that the language of sacrifice was well understood in the first century. It seems the ideas associated with it inevitably rubbed on to Christianity a little. But secondly, there has been a problem of translation. If you look at the modern Bible translations of St John's epistle you will see that they do not use the word 'propitiation'. The Revised Standard version refers instead to 'expiation'. That's something that makes amends. The New English Bible says simply that Jesus is the remedy for the defilement of our sins. The word 'remedy' has no association with an angry God demanding payment. It is much closer to the idea of Jesus being a sacrifice in the sense of a loving gift. St John says that God gave his son because he loved the world so much. As for Jesus, 'Greater love hath no man', he said, 'than he lay down his life for his friends.' In that sense certainly his death was a sacrifice.

9 November 1985

Durham Blues

I think I am beginning to despair about the controversy over Bishop Jenkins of Durham. The thing that is currently depressing me most is that the argument in the church has come to a head yet again in the days just before the most marvellous moment in the whole of the Christian year. The moment when Christians in many parts of the world proclaim their joyful faith that Christ is Risen. This week, yet again, I saw a report claiming in passing that Bishop Jenkins did not believe in the Resurrection. Now I don't share all Bishop Jenkins's views. Yet I know for a fact that throughout this year, he has declared again and again, passionately, that he does believe in the Resurrection. How is it that after all this time, he is still being misquoted? The point is that the question of whether Christ is Risen is *not* at issue. Every single bishop in the Church of England believes that Christ is Risen and that the message of Easter is that life and love can conquer death and suffering.

Equally every single bishop in the Church of England agrees with Paul's description of the risen body in his first letter to the Corinthians, chapter 15. Paul wrote this letter in response to people who had kept coming to him, asking him 'How are the dead raised up?' It's a silly question, he answers, but nevertheless he goes on to try to satisfy them with some sort of reply.

The seed you sow does not come to life unless it has first died; and what you sow is not the body that shall be, but a naked grain, perhaps of wheat, or of some other kind; and God clothes it with the body of his choice, each seed with its own particular body. All flesh is not the same flesh: there is flesh of men, flesh of beasts, of birds, and of fishes – all different. There are heavenly bodies and earthly bodies; and the splendour of the heavenly bodies is one thing, the splendour of the earthly, another . . . So it is with the resurrection of the dead. What is sown in the earth as a perishable thing is raised imperishable. Sown in humiliation, it is raised in glory; sown in weakness, it is raised in power; sown as an animal body, it is raised as a spiritual body.

Flesh and blood, Paul goes on to say, will not inherit the kingdom of heaven. It is our spiritual bodies that will be raised.

It is this chapter in St Paul that Bishop Jenkins says summarises his own understanding of the resurrection of Christ. And he maintains that his belief that Christ was raised up does not depend on whether or not Christ's physical body remained in the tomb.

But what about the gospel accounts that describe how Mary Magdalene and other women went to visit the tomb on Easter morning and discovered it empty? Is Bishop Jenkins suggesting that the gospel writers were liars? No, he says, of course he is not describing them as liars. He believes that they wrote those accounts down like that because they believed them to be true. But he points out that they were written probably thirty or more years after the events described, and the narratives differ from each other in a number of important details. Could it be that the stories came to be told that way because that was the best way of communicating that God had transformed the hearts and minds of the disciples?

Bishop Jenkins says he doesn't know the answer, because we don't know exactly how the gospels came to be written. But some Christians feel that if you don't accept the accounts of the

Empty Tomb, you are only saying Christ lives on in the same way as you might say 'Che Guevara lives on.' Bishop Jenkins denies this. For he believes that God raised up Christ and that this proclaims that love can triumph over sin, that life can triumph over death. And if we really believe that, he says, our lives must be changed because God then uses us to stand alongside all those who are lost or sad or without hope.

He explained all this in his diocesan letter released a few days ago. Most of it was an inspiring call to the people in his diocese to think about what it means for the people of God to live out the good news of the resurrection. Yet most of the reports concentrated only on the sentences which spoke of his uncertainty whether or not the tomb itself was empty. Hardly a word about his understanding of what the resurrection meant, even though the letter was really about this

Thank God that tomorrow when Christians know once again in their hearts that Christ is Risen, none of these misunderstandings will any longer matter.

6 April 1985

Best Bible Bits

I've just been on holiday for a couple of weeks, and in between dodging downpours in Devon, hill walking and picking bilberries, I've been reading parts of that majestic and somewhat shocking bestseller, the Old Testament. I first embarked on it seriously when I was sixteen. And within a few weeks I was in a state of considerable muddle – entranced and excited by some of it, angered and disturbed by other sections. I still find many of the stories compelling – King David's secret fixing of the murder of Uriah the Hittite so he can marry Uriah's wife Bathsheba whom he, David, had made pregnant is pure Mafia.

You remember that David has his come-uppance through Nathan the Prophet. Nathan goes to see David and tells him of a very rich man in his kingdom, owner of many herds, who nevertheless is so mean that he has stolen the only lamb of a poor man. David gets into a frightful sweat about this, declares that the unjust man who did this must surely die. The next line is one of the most dramatic in the whole of the Bible. Nathan swings round on David – you can imagine him fixing him with his eye and pointing a searing finger at him – and says, '*Thou* art the man!' All that comes in the second book of Samuel, chapter 12. But some other chunks of the Old Testament are rather less clear in their moral message. Not to say downright sickening.

One of the nineteenth-century missionaries to South Africa was John William Colenso, Bishop of Natal. When he was in Zululand, the horror with which some of the most devout and intelligent Africans questioned the truth of the first five books of the Bible confirmed his own doubts of parts of the records. Translating with the help of a Zulu scholar, he came to the passage in Exodus, chapter 21, which says, 'If a man smite his servant, or his maid, with a rod, and he die under his hand; he shall be surely punished . . . If he continue [to live] a day or two, he shall not be punished; for he is his money.' The bishop wrote that he never forgot the revulsion with which the Zulu translator heard these words, said to be uttered by the same great and gracious being whom he was teaching him to trust in and adore. The Zulu's whole soul revolted against the notion that the great and blessed God, the merciful father of all mankind, would speak of a servant or a maid as mere money and allow a horrible crime to go unpunished, because the victim of the brutal treatment had survived a few hours.

So how do believers today cope with such texts? Well, some don't. There is a tendency in many churches today to drop the Old Testament reading altogether, and so avoid difficult passages that way. A more honest approach might be to include the readings but make sure that the sermon or the address puts them in their historical context.

We tend to forget, as one scholar has pointed out, that the Israelites in those days lived among nations who justified stealing, authorised infanticide, legalised the murder of aged parents and associated lust with worship. Ancient Israelite codes rejected these and taught that people should not be imprisoned for debt. They led the prosperous to lend without interest and to care for widows and orphans and strangers. Many a minute safeguard was laid down – like the return of a debtor's garment at nightfall to save him from suffering during the chill nights.

The ancient Israelites were no doubt barbarous in many things, childish in others, but their belief in one God and the general principles of their moral code, as it developed over the centuries, were singular in humanity compared with their contemporaries.

For it did develop. The religious understanding of progressive revelation was once explained to me like this. Imagine a room filled with beautiful furniture. In one corner of the room there is a flickering candle. Thousands of years ago, people saw some of the furniture clearly. But the far side of the room was still in total darkness. In between were some pieces of furniture which in the gloom were mistaken. When more light entered the room, people saw that what was once thought to be, say, a table was really something quite different. The beautiful furniture is there all the time but gradually with the help of prophets and others we see it more truly as it really is. The Old Testament is an account of how people, in the dim mists of prehistory, saw the room then. But we shouldn't be too worried if they got some of it wrong.

9 August 1986

We Believe . . .

The Church of England is actually talking about *God*. Surely not, you cry. There must be some mistake. Surely you mean building appeals, or proportional representation, or Desmond Tutu, or relations with the Roman Catholics. No, it really is God. I have in my hand a booklet called *We Believe in God*. And not only does it passionately and evidently mean what it says, but it explores what *kind* of God and how he works in our world today.

It comes, with the authority of the house of bishops, from that august body the Doctrine Commission, whose current membership, incidentally, includes two *women* theologians. The booklet was published yesterday, and as you may have already heard on broadcasts or seen in newspaper reports, it explores belief in God in a way that both challenges and responds to the thinking of today's world.

There's so much good stuff in it that it's hard to know where to start. For the most heartening thing about it, is that it does try to answer *real* questions. It speaks to people who've suffered tragedy in their personal lives and who ask how God, who's supposed to be all-powerful, can allow such misery. It speaks to anyone who's read certain Bible stories about a God who sounds so vengeful that they've felt sickened, and put the Bible down. It speaks to people who quite rightly have been revolted by the way in past centuries there has been no social evil, no form of injustice, which has not been sanctified in some way or another by religious sentiment. And it speaks to those who think that the discoveries of modern science have ruled out for ever belief in God.

At the heart of the report is the idea of God waiting on the response of human beings. His hands and feet in the world are our hands and feet. It goes on to suggest that faith is not a prepackaged set of rules and doctrines whose meaning is set in concrete. Instead it's the idea of faith as a journey towards God. Religion, it says, *like* science, is a voyage of discovery.

The parallel with science yields some fascinating ideas. The theologians say that in science there are continuing and genuine gains in human understanding. But these are combined, as all scientists know, with accounts of reality which are undoubtedly incomplete, provisional, and open to correction. So scientists are constantly trying to sift the grain from the chaff. Religion, the theologians say, is similar. All pictures about God are necessarily incomplete and open to correction. But gradually over the centuries, the church, like the scientists, proceeds on its journey towards a better understanding of reality. Some of the old ideas and images drop away, but the *grain* from the past is preserved. So today's Christians, like dwarfs on the shoulders of giants, can see more and further than Christians in earlier centuries. That's not because they are keener and taller, but because of the greatness by which they are carried.

To some Christians this idea of the church always open to correction may feel threatening. But for many believers and those hovering on the edge of belief, this scholarly and moving book will help them closer to God. For that, much thanks.

6 June 1987

11

ODDS
AND ENDS

Poles Apart

Downtown Vancouver is an elegant city with sky-scrapers reflecting each other in their glass walls, broad high-ways lined with trees, attractive – though expensive – shops, and, it seems, only a few drunks on the streets. It also has what the postcards claim to be the largest suspension bridge in the British Empire, by which I think they mean the Common-wealth! Take a bus from the main street across Lionsgate Bridge with its spectacular view of the city spread out below and in less than an hour you can be swimming in a lake cooled by melting ice and surrounded by dense forest clinging to the side of one of the north shore mountains.

In that range of rugged British Columbian peaks not so very long ago, the native Indians of Canada got on with their hunting and salmon fishing, undisturbed by the white, should I say paleface, visitors. Today that culture is pretty much ruined. One day this week, I took a taxi downtown and the driver, a man of about fifty who took up cab-driving when he got sick of journalism, got talking about the Indians. 'I hate them,' he said. 'They are dirty and they smell. The government pays out welfare cheques once a month on a Wednesday and every month there are drunk Indians round town.'

Yet right now galleries all round the Pacific are buying up Indian art and in parks and museums and even on university campuses on this north-west coast of Canada, you can regularly see symbols of Indian culture. The symbols are tall trunks of western red cedar, carved with brightly painted, highly stylised images of birds, animals and people. And they are, of course, totem poles.

Totem poles are rather difficult to explain. In one sense they are like a Picasso painting. You can't look at them and ask what they mean. The meaning is what they say to you personally and how you respond to them. Someone said that you have to let the images sink into your dreaming, but what is clear is that they were not intended to represent demons or gods. They were never worshipped. But they did have deep religious significance. They are made up of symbolic figures commemorating a vision, an event or a death. Each crest figure is easily distinguished. The beaver always had a recognisable tail. The thunderbird a carved beak and horns. Each animal carved represents something different and without knowing the life-story of the owner it's impossible to read a pole completely, except as a list of crests. But the beings represented on the poles are those beings who in mythical times either became or were met by the ancestors of the group that later adopted them as crests. So, for example, some Indian families claim as their sign the thunderbird who descended from the sky to take off his animal clothing and became their human ancestor. Rich and important families claim many crests. Both private and public myths told of an age before the world became as it is now, an age when divisions between animals, humans and spirits had not yet been created and each could transform itself from one form to another. All realms – water, earth, sky and the land of the dead – were connected by beings who could pass between them and it's this that the totem poles report.

Very broadly there are three types of pole. First of all the memorial pole, portraying families, crests and stories. These were erected to commemorate special events like battles or significant dreams or visions. I suppose our nearest equivalent would be a war memorial. Then there is the mortuary pole, raised as a grave-post over an important leader. And then there are the house poles. These had a hole cut into them to make the front entrance of the house which was built on to one side, with the top of the pole towering above. There are also, as a sort of addendum, welcome poles – figures placed on the beach to welcome guests arriving by canoe.

Here in Canada there is a growing movement among Indians and others to value and respect native Canadian culture once more. There are people like the taxi-driver to whom it's a romantic dream trying pointlessly to bring back what has gone. But as the Pacific becomes polluted by nuclear testing, there are Christians and others here who feel that the Indian vision of the oneness of creation has closer links with Christianity than some aspects of technical experiment.

6 August 1983

Dressed to Kill

It occurred to me the other day what a very ambivalent attitude the British have towards their clergy. Anti-clericalism has never run as wild here as it has in France, but everybody knows a joke about a vicar, in the same way that everyone knows a joke about a mother-in-law, and comic satire has long been the British response to the naïve other-worldliness of some clerics. In fact, there's a tension between our amusement at clerical goings-on and our respect for the faith the clergy represent. This ambivalence was displayed in a memorable headline in the London *Evening News* in March 1980. It was the day the present Archbishop of Canterbury was enthroned. The front page was divided between that and the second lead, a story about the dramatic sentencing of a gang who had ambushed their rivals with guns and knives. On one side of the page was a particularly formal and lugubrious picture of the archbishop looking out from underneath his spectacles and also from underneath a very large bishop's mitre. The headline beside him was 'Hell's Angel Gets Fifteen Years'.

Heaven knows, some ecclesiastical traditions and ways of going on appear to many sensible people who are neither totally deaf nor blind to religious feeling, to be pretty silly. Or, if not that, then pretty much obscure. Take, for example, clerical dress. Why do ministers wear mitres and cassocks and surplices and the rest? What *is* it about?

Well, for a start it is almost certainly not about imitating the early church. It seems that for the first 500 years or so of the church's life, the clergy wore the same clothes as everyone else. St Augustine – the first Archbishop of Canterbury – apparently had no priestly clothing, and St Ambrose says fairly plainly that we should recognise a bishop by his charity and by his role and not by his clothes.

The change came about after the Roman Empire was threatened by invasions from the barbarians. People gradually adopted the invaders' style of short clothes and abandoned the traditional Roman and oriental style of clothing. But the clergy continued to wear the long wide robes, and have done so with variations ever since.

Why, you may ask, have they in this country adopted so many layers of clothing? I wish I could give you a wonderfully inspiring theological reply. In fact the reason it seems is down-to-earth – the churches were always so very cold. At a time when church central heating hadn't been dreamt of, clergy often wore a furry garment called a *pelliceum*. The choir dress worn over the top of this had to be bulky enough to cover the fur. That's why the surplice is the shape it is and why it has the name it does. Surplice is a corruption of '*superpelliceum*', meaning on top of the fur.

It all seems a long way from the church up the road in twentieth-century Britain. I suppose the real question is whether ornaments like these are any longer appropriate? For some people, the argument of tradition is sufficient to continue with them. Besides, they say, the garments glorify not the wearer, but God, and they contribute more to the drama and the significance of worship than does, say, an ordinary lounge suit. In any case, all sorts of other professions – nurses, police, judges – have uniforms. Why not clergy? Other Christians, however, like the Quakers, are not convinced and have never worn special vestments. I personally would be sad never to be able to recognise by their dress a nun or a priest in public. But maybe the church should occasionally spare a thought for those people who find archaic clothes and ritual either totally obscure or even funny. They can certainly create yet another barrier between people's Christian interest and the institutional church.

20 August 1983

Noah's Lark

I see that the search for Noah's Ark has gathered steam yet again. This summer another team of intrepid American explorers has been struggling up Mount Ararat in eastern Turkey, looking for bits of wood and pitch. And last weekend, the team's leader, Mr Marvin Steffins, told a news conference in Ankara that he was confident that a boat-shaped formation found a third of the way up the mountain would prove to be Noah's Ark. On Wednesday, Mr Steffins was about to board an airliner in Istanbul for New York, with 8½ pounds of relics tidily packed in his luggage, when the Turkish police stepped in, held him for three hours and confiscated his discoveries. They were whisked off for a preliminary analysis by the Istanbul Archaeology Museum, and within hours Turkey's Culture and Tourism Minister was declaring that the samples had no historic value whatsoever. They were, he said, only rocks and soil, not wood. Nevertheless the samples are to undergo further tests to determine their content and approximate age.

For some of you, it may come as a shock that anyone could imagine that relics of the ark exist. Many Christians regard the account of Noah, not as a description of historical fact, but a story told to express the religious conviction that God saves those who follow his ways and live a good life. But people like

Mr Steffins and the one-time astronaut, Colonel James Irwin, believe that somewhere beneath the iron-hard ice and perpetual snows of Ararat lie the remains of a boat about half the size of an ocean-going liner. And it was into that boat, they think, that Noah collected pairs of every species of animal and bird life to save them from the flood that engulfed the world.

Narrative traditions about an ancient flood certainly exist throughout the world, starting from about 2300 BC. Ararat is given as the resting place of an ark in the holy books of three great religions and mountain-tops do reveal traces of marine life. But marine archaeologists say that originally *all* rocks lay beneath water. Other archaeologists say that there's no evidence of a universal flood, though various regions do have traces of floods at different times. Some Christians believe the flood took place round about 2500 BC, but the city of Jericho, for instance, whose foundations have been traced back 9,000 years, reveals, I'm told, no flood signs in that whole period.

Nevertheless the ark story does have a powerful hold on the Christian imagination. The word 'nave' – which refers to the central part of a church building – comes from the Latin *navis*, meaning a boat. Moreover Ararat has attracted many hermits and holy men. And there are stories of the Armenian people who once lived around Ararat taking their sons on pilgrimage to the site of the ark's resting place. Only a few years ago, just before his death in 1972, one elderly Armenian then living in the United States, described his childhood ascent of the mountain with his uncle. The atmosphere was, he said, cold and misty, the ark rested on a huge rock, bluish-green in colour, with one side on the edge of a steep cliff. The ark was very long and rectangular with a flat bottom, and a nearly flat roof.

Not surprising then that in the last 150 years a number of western explorers have braved the cold and the mist to search the arid, desolate landscape. The Turkish name of the mountain means 'Mount of Agony'. One explorer has said it's justly named. The air is so rarefied that at night you may hallucinate. It's hard to take oxygen equipment because the mountain is so difficult to climb.

And the search even with the help of aerial photographs seems like looking for pins at the bottom of the sea. Ararat has two peaks seven miles apart. An ice-cap is said to cover about twenty square miles. Tradition has indicated certain areas rather than others, but who knows what may have happened in the course of centuries of weathering. Originally the ark – if there was one – must have landed near the top, but snowfalls and slides may have brought it down thousands of feet, and scattered and covered over any broken debris.

But Mr Steffins is talking about returning next year for a fifth expedition. The Turkish press no doubt will continue to scoff, and the Russians to glower. After all, Ararat stands on the Turkish-Soviet frontier and has a fine view of Soviet territory. Dark suspicions float in some Soviet minds that all these exercises are a useful cover for electronic American surveillance. They find it hard to believe that anyone could take the Ark story seriously.

1 September 1984

Divine Wrong

Three hundred years ago this month a splendid banquet was held in Westminster Hall. At one private table for two no fewer than 175 dishes were served. Among them were stags' tongues, cold mince pies, twelve lobsters, twenty-four puffins and a lemon jelly. The gourmet diners were a king and queen, James II and his wife Mary of Modena, who an hour or two before had been anointed and crowned with sumptuous magnificence in the presence of the court across the road in Westminster Abbey.

James believed himself to be king by divine right. He hoped that in a few years' time, he could help England return to the fold of Rome and the universal Catholic church, from which in his view it had sadly and wilfully strayed 150 years before. Yet only three years later, James's hopes were in ruins. He himself

had fled London, leaving his country to the rule of his Protestant daughter Mary and his son-in-law William of Orange
from the Netherlands. James spent the rest of his life in melan-
choly exile in France.

A few weeks ago I trekked down to the Reading Room of the
British Museum Library to look up the official contemporary
account of the coronation – who sat where, what they wore,
what the choirs sang. It described, in fact, a national fantasy.
James knew well that the aim of a coronation is to reveal and
sum up the significance of a historical process through the ages.
He was so keen to have a truly magnificent coronation that he's
said to have given attention to nothing else for some weeks
beforehand. The music and the liturgy emphasised again and
again that this man was God's anointed king, chosen to rule
over the nation in the ways of justice and peace.

Biblically, it's all carefully traced back to the first book of
Kings, chapter 1, where King David, as he lies dying, calls on
Zadok the priest and Nathan the prophet to anoint his son
Solomon King of Israel. But despite the pomp and grandeur of
that seventeenth-century service, a Monty Python element took
over. The crown didn't fit. It had been made for the larger head
of Charles II and was too big for James. The Keeper of the
Robes, Henry Sidney, held it up, saying pleasantly that it
wasn't the first time his family had supported the crown. How
ironic that within three years, Henry Sidney had deserted
James and gone to support William of Orange.

The man who anointed and crowned James was the Archbishop
of Canterbury, William Sancroft. Three years later in 1688 James
had Sancroft and six other bishops sent to the Tower for refusing
to follow his wishes. The cause? Religion, of course.

Sancroft and the other bishops had hoped that the king
would practise his Roman Catholicism discreetly in the years to
come, with political good sense. But James preferred instead to
do what he thought was right. He could not believe that it was
right to ban Catholics from public office, or to fine people for
not attending Church of England services. So he began to
appoint Roman Catholics to official posts, released dissenters

from prison, and took steps to declare liberty of conscience. None of this today seems very radical to us. But in the seventeenth century, not an age of tolerance, people believed it foreshadowed the return to Catholic domination and persecution of Anglicans. When in 1688 Archbishop Sancroft and six of his colleagues refused to read from their pulpits a declaration of indulgence on religious matters, they were arrested on a charge of seditious libel. The jury, in a sensational trial, found them not guilty. But when the queen gave birth to a son and heir, and the Pope was invited to be a godfather, national patience ran out. James had had his chance and muffed it.

After William and Mary took power, laws were introduced preventing a Roman Catholic from becoming monarch ever again. The Act of Settlement of 1701 prevents those in the line of succession to the throne from even marrying a 'papist' without prejudicing their own rights to succession. Some members of the Church of England today feel these words are an unnecessary affront to the Roman Catholic community. They argue that all that's necessary is for the children of any such marriage to be baptised and brought up within the Church of England. But James's unfortunate reign bit so deep into the national memory that even 300 years later, most people, it seems, still prefer to leave things as they are, Act of Settlement and all.

13 April 1985

Our Doris

What happens after death? That's the million dollar question. It affects not only how we live now, but how we die, and that's one of the reasons why several thousand people came last weekend [30–31 August] in coach-loads to the Wembley Conference Centre. They were there for an audience with the medium Doris Stokes.* Doris comes from Grantham,

---

* Doris Stokes herself 'passed over' in May 1987.

home too of the Prime Minister. She's the first medium to have appeared at the London Palladium, she's been at the Sydney Opera House, appeared on *Desert Island Discs* and written five books which are said to have sold 1.25 million copies. And she talks to what she says are the 'so-called' dead.

For £6 you could get a comfortable seat in the carpeted auditorium. The audience included teenagers, young couples as well as older people. But the vast majority were women. On stage were flowers and a red velvet armchair. Before it began we heard records of songs like Jim Reeves's 'I Love You Because'. Then Doris arrived, with white hair and gold shoes and wearing a long flowing chiffon dress in pastel colours. The lights stayed up.

Doris talks to people on the other side rather as a cheerful manageress of a pub keeps in order the lads who are trying to pull her leg and jump the queue in ordering drinks. The difference is that it's as if they're talking to her down a very crackly telephone line. 'What's that you're saying, dearie?' she'll say. Sometimes she will mishear things. Last week she talked only to *men* on the other side. The messages to people still in this life were all comforting ones. Rather like the ones they used to broadcast on *Two-Way Family Favourites* years ago. Messages like 'I'm all right, give her my dearest love.'

There is no doubt that many people in the audience genuinely felt that she was in touch with the other side. But just recently Doris Stokes came under attack by a stage magician who claimed that she was just using ordinary effects to trick the audience. If you were sceptical then you could certainly develop a strong case. In an audience so large it's a fair bet, for instance, that there's someone who has a dead loved one called 'John', that someone would have some contact with the Co-op or Marks & Spencer. Many of the questions are open-ended. 'Who is Fred?' she'll say. And someone will tell her and give her some more clues to work on. Some of it she gets plain wrong. She was insistent that the sum of £252 meant something. No one in the huge audience could tune into that. Every now and again she would say a name and the person she was talking to

would say, 'That's my sister' or 'You mean my brother-in-law.'
But does she really display any more than luck, a strong in-
tuition and a wide knowledge of life and people?

Well, whatever your viewpoint it seems to me that she was
really dealing with love and forgiveness. One woman in the
audience there spoke of how her father-in-law had been left by
his wife shortly before he died, and it had taken the family a
fortnight to find the body. What Doris Stokes did in conven-
tional religious terms was to give her absolution. She accepted
the woman's sense of guilt, told her that the father-in-law was
saying it was all right and that he had died quickly and not in
pain. She helped her to forgive herself, and to go on with her
life. This was a frequent message in her counselling – 'You must
now get on with your life,' she said. 'It's all right.'

How can this be wrong or bad? – some people ask. Well, some
psychologists believe that instead of being helped to let go of
their dead ones and carry on with their life, people become
obsessed with trying to get in touch with them. Once they have
had one message they keep coming to these sessions in the hope
of having more messages. But my impression was that she was
actually helping people to move on with their life. Certainly she
behaved like no stage magician. The tone of what she said and
did was compassionate and sensitive.

From the Christian point of view the messages brought no
sense of the great bliss of the Christian vision of heaven. But as
one member of the audience said to me, they speak to where
people are. And people don't understand love in the abstract.
We know it most directly through contact with those we love
and who love us, spoken in everyday language we can understand. And even if some of the messages sound to the outsider
banal, they do speak of love.

The overwhelming impression I had from this meeting was
the sense of need. It was a reminder that we all need to have and
to give love and forgiveness. And it's better to have and give
them now rather than when it feels too late and too much was
left unsaid.

6 September 1986